ROBERT BROWNING

A
BROWNING PRIMER

BY

ESTHER PHŒBE DEFRIES

WITH AN INTRODUCTION BY

Dr. F. J. FURNIVALL

KENNIKAT PRESS
Port Washington, N. Y./London

CONTENTS

N.B.—The Poems are discussed according to their arrangements in the sixteen volume edition of 1889 (Smith, Elder & Co.), which was revised by Browning himself.

A BROWNING PRIMER

First published in 1892
Reissued in 1970 by Kennikat Press
Library of Congress Catalog Card No: 70-103182
SBN 8046-0819-9

Manufactured by Taylor Publishing Company   Dallas, Texas

INTRODUCTION

THE Browning Society always wanted a Shilling Primer to Browning's works; and when a Shilling Selection from those works was promised, the need for a cheap Primer became more urgent. Miss Defries, now Mrs. Leon, kindly undertook to write the Primer, and Messrs. Swan Sonnenschein & Co. agreed to publish it.

The selection in the shilling volume is badly made, inasmuch as the careless chooser of the poems has (1) put in several third-rate and un-interesting poems of Browning's, and left out some of his best, like *Fra Lippo, Caliban, Count Gismond, Up at a Villa, Home Thoughts;* and has (2) confused the time-order of the pieces, putting (for instance) *Porphyria's Lover*, of 1836, between two poems of 1855, *The Statue and the Bust* and *Childe Rolande;* and *Pisgah Sights*, of 1849, between two groups of poems of 1876. But the little book does contain some of the poet's most characteristic works, and has introduced him to many thousand readers who knew little or nothing of him before its appearance. Some of these at least will be glad to see the general sketch of Browning and his poems that Mrs. Leon has drawn up.

For myself, when urging on folk the study of Browning, I always admit his faults, his often failure in moulding his verse, his want of lucidity, his habit of going off at tangents, &c.; but I insist that for manliness, strength, vividness, penetration, humour, buoyancy, characterisation, insight into music and art, he has no equal in modern poetry. He is not for lovers of the commonplace, the pretty, or the sentimental, for drawing-room misses or namby-pamby dawdlers. He is for men and women with the thews of mind and soul which move the world and raise their possessors to the highest level that mortals can attain. He is worthy of the earnest study of all earnest folk; and to them I commend him.

F. J. FURNIVALL.

27th October, 1892.

AUTHOR'S PREFACE

———•———

BEFORE introducing this little book to the public, I should like to thank Dr. Furnivall, who first suggested to me the idea of writing it—not only for the idea, but for the kind use he has allowed me of his Browning Bibliography, and of his books. My thanks are also due to the works of Mrs. Orr, Mr. Arthur Symons, Mr. Nettleship, and Mr. Fotheringham, which have been of much service to me.

This book tries to give a first sketch of Browning's poetry. It is not meant for readers to whom the poems are already familiar, but for those who are as yet unacquainted with them. To such readers critical assistance would be almost premature, and I have in-

tentionally preferred to write in the most con-
ventional and non-critical spirit, hoping no more
than that this book may act as a sign-post to
the beauties which are to be found in the poems,
and to some slight extent as a guide to the way
in which difficulties, which are sometimes over-
stated, may be overcome.

My aim is to induce a few more English men
and women to read Browning in a spirit of gratitude and affection, in order that they may share
the pleasure, and perhaps the help, which such
reading has given to many besides me.

E. PH. D.

ROBERT BROWNING.

CHAPTER I.

THE LIFE OF BROWNING.

ROBERT BROWNING was born at Camberwell, May 7th, 1812. The mixed nationality of which he comes forms an important and interesting clue to the broadness of his ideas and sympathies. His father's mother was a Creole of St. Kitts; his mother's mother a Scotchwoman. She married a Scotch-German mariner, William Wiedermann, and of this marriage was born the poet's mother, Sarianna Wiedermann. His father, also Robert Browning, was a clerk in the Bank of England, but the occupation was an uncongenial one, and he determined that his son should follow the bent of his inclinations, whithersoever they might lead him. A loveless and unhappy childhood had pre-disposed the elder Browning towards making his children's lives as happy as possible.

From early childhood Browning displayed a restless, energetic, and eminently sensitive disposition. This last quality he seems to have inherited from his mother, a delicate woman of nervous constitution. From her also he derived his love and appreciation of music. His intimate

A

knowledge of animal life and of inanimate nature also began in childhood. At ten years of age he was sent to the Rev. Thomas Ready's school at Peckham, for which he had been prepared by the Misses Ready. He remained there until he was fourteen, then for three years studied at home with a tutor, and afterwards went to University College, Gower Street, for a short time. This somewhat unsystematic course of education had comparatively little influence on his later life, and his extensive knowledge is almost entirely the result of his own extensive reading and research. His poetic tendency showed itself while he was very young, an enthusiastic but short-lived admiration for Byron giving place at the age of fourteen to the deep and lasting impression which the works of Keats, and still more of Shelley, made upon him. *Popularity*, written nearly forty years after, is a tribute to Keats ; while we find evidence of his devotion to Shelley in *Pauline*, *Sordello*, *Memorabilia*, and *Cenciaja*. His first publication was in 1833, when *Pauline* appeared anonymously. Two years later *Paracelsus* appeared, duly signed by its author. About this time Browning was introduced to Macready. Keenly interested in acting and actors, Browning very gladly undertook at Macready's request to write a play for him. *Strafford* (1837) was the result, and might have proved a success had Miss Helen Faucit and Macready received better support from the rest of the actors ; but the inability of the management from lack of funds to mount or cast it properly caused it to be withdrawn after five performances. It is practically impossible to trace the growth of Browning's power and genius as the years rolled on, for although *The Ring and the Book* is justly considered his greatest achievement, yet there is little that excels *Pippa Passes,* which was written at the age of twenty-nine. The nine years following the production of *Strafford* saw the publication of *Sordello* and the series of BELLS AND POMEGRANATES, containing the remainder of the plays, DRAMATIC ROMANCES and DRAMATIC LYRICS. In 1844 he made the acquaintance of the poetess Elizabeth Barrett, whose works he already knew and admired, and on September 12th, 1846, they were secretly married. With his marriage came the necessity to live abroad for the benefit of Mrs. Browning's health, and thence sprang the indelible influence which Italy exercised upon his work. In March, 1849, a son was born to them, but joy and sorrow came hand in hand, for Browning's mother died on the day of his son's birth. Browning's devotion to his mother was very great. But in the love of his wife he was comforted for his mother's death, and for twelve more years supreme happiness reigned in the home of the poet husband and wife. In 1861, however, death bore away his "perfect wife," leaving him with a life-long grief which would have completely crushed a weaker man. For his son's sake, however, he conquered the gloom which threatened to surround his life, and at once devoted himself to his paternal duties. From this time Browning established himself in London in "the third house by the bridge,"[1] No. 19 Warwick Crescent, Maida Hill; and on the death of their father in 1866, his sister, Miss Sarianna Browning, made her home with him. From 1861 till 1864 he published nothing, but the appearance in 1864 of MEN AND WOMEN proves that he was not idle in the interval. This was followed four

---

[1] Cf. *How it Strikes a Contemporary.*

years later (1868-69) by one of the greatest products of English literature, THE RING AND THE BOOK. In June, 1867, the University of Oxford conferred the degree of M.A. upon him, and in the following October he was made Honorary Fellow of Balliol College. On the death of Mr. John Stuart Mill in 1868, and again nine years later, he was offered, but on each occasion declined, the Lord Rectorship of the University of St. Andrews. In 1879 he received the degree of LL.D. at Cambridge, and in 1882 that of D.C.L. of Oxford.

In 1887 he moved from Warwick Crescent to De Vere Gardens, Kensington, a house altogether better suited to his requirements. In October of this year Mr. Barrett Browning married, and it was at the house of his dearly loved son and daughter, the Palazzo Rezzonico, Venice, that in 1889 the poet "passed to where beyond these voices there is peace."

CHAPTER II.

RELIGION.—" God's in his heaven—
All's right with the world ! "

THESE simple words, put into the mouth of the little peasant-girl Pippa, may fairly be said to strike the key-note of Browning's faith. His religion was undoubtedly Christianity, though it appears to a great extent to verge on Theism, and, but for his wife's influence, might possibly have become so. As it was, however, he accepted in the broad sense the ideal spirit of Christianity, and in strength and sympathy he has interpreted its spiritual and human depths. He was a man of much faith. He had faith in God, His love and power, and with this primary faith he included faith in friendship and human love, faith in high ideals, faith in the great principles of Art and Science, and he held that this comprehensive faith had its use and even its origin in the conflict of good with evil in man's soul. Browning depicts these conflicts vividly, often letting evil gain the apparent mastery, but invariably showing that faith rightly used would have been capable of reversing the victory. He rejected all certainty in religious dogma, and only believed in Christ as a Divine mystery, not as a definite fact about which all that can be known is known. He felt that if religion can be definitely asserted in a cut-and-dried

5

form for all time, progress in spiritual life must end, and
stagnation ensue. It was his belief that spiritual life
needs uncertainty to develop it, and forbids any sense of
finality. Love and self-sacrifice for God and man form
the sole channel through which humanity can reach the
Deity, although his creed invested the Deity himself
with no human emotions. He believed that life does
not cease with what we know as death, but how or in
what changed form it continues to exist he felt was
the Divine mystery. His almost prophetic belief in this
after-life was, moreover, not so much the result of blind,
unthinking faith, as of logical reasoning, based upon the
mainspring of his life—love. He could not explain, but yet
felt, the need of loving and of being loved, and it is from
this strong religion of love that his world-wide sympathies
spring. They are not derived from the mere scientific
interest of a psychologist, but from the genuine belief
that all men are brothers, and form with him the great
family of God. It is in this self-same spirit that Browning exhibits his sympathy for other religions. No better
expression of religious toleration can be found than his
denunciation in *Holy Cross Day* of Jewish perse-
cutions, together with the poet's own prose comment
at the end, "The present Pope abolished this *bad
business* of the sermon. R.B." As for his feelings
towards Roman Catholicism, we know that Browning
treated the subject in such a way as to win a favourable
review from Cardinal Wiseman, who is said to have been
the original of "Bishop Blougram." As the poet
grew older he rejected more and more all forms and
restrictions of religious belief, but it is remarkable that
throughout all variations of style, subject, and quality, the
faith to which we have alluded consistently permeates his

work from his earliest fragment to his latest epilogue. Perhaps the most nearly absolute confession of his form of faith occurs in *La Saisiaz*, but the consistency of his deep and unvarying trust in good and God may be illustrated by the following quotations from (1) *Prospice (Dram. Pers.* 1864), and from (2) the *Epilogue* to ASOLANDO, his latest volume.

(1) " For sudden the worst turns the best to the brave,
    The black minute's at end,
And the elements' rage, the fiend-voices that rave,
    Shall dwindle, shall blend,
Shall change, shall become first a peace out of pain,
    Then a light, then thy breast,
O thou soul of my soul ! I shall clasp thee again
    And with God be the rest !"

(2) " One who never turned his back but marched breast
    forward,
    Never doubted clouds would break,
Never dreamed, though right was worsted, wrong
    would triumph,
Held we fall to rise, are baffled to fight better,
    Sleep to wake."

SUBJECT.—Browning has, out of the many subjects open to poetic treatment, deliberately chosen for his own the human soul. In a note dedicating *Sordello* to Mr. J. Milsand of Dijon, he writes, ". . . . . my stress lay on the incidents in the development of a soul : little else is worth study. I at least always thought so." Everywhere all other interests are subordinated to the human. Man has been created with innumerable possibilities in his soul; according to Browning the poet's mission is the development of these possibilities in indi-

vidual men and women in all the conditions and circumstances of life. The necessary consequence of dealing with
so difficult a subject is that the resulting poetry cannot be
carelessly read, and Browning protests against the use of
his poetry as a substitute for a cigar after dinner. Browning believed that the individual soul is of all-importance
in the plan of life ; that the final value and result of life is
found, not in outward action, but within ourselves. In
pursuance of this belief he shows us the emotions and
motives of the soul, instead of the action to which these
lead. He takes a human soul, apparently possessing in
itself but little interest, and invests it with interest by
placing it in some critical situation where a single step
towards good or evil will decide its ultimate fate. Then
he proceeds to analyse each conflicting emotion in
such a way that the final result seems the only natural
and possible one. It is this result which gives to his
dramas their special character. They are, to a great
extent, dramas of thought, not of action. Their chief
interest lies in the emotions which they present, not in the
events which occur. Browning accordingly makes very
frequent use of monologue. He makes the character under dissection explain itself. In some cases deliberately,
and in others unconsciously, it reveals its very inmost soul,
so that we realise the fitness of all that had at first seemed
incongruous. No writer has made so constant or better
use of monologue. He employs it both in his dramas
and his shorter poems.

PAINTING AND MUSIC.—Although Browning's life
was given up to poetry, he did not allow his knowledge
of music and art to be idle. Browning stands acknowledged as the poet of painting and of music. He was

the first among poets to interpret the hidden depths of art and its spiritual relation to humanity.   He speaks not as the poet dwelling on an unfamiliar theme, but as the artist himself might speak, could he express his inmost soul in verse.   In the poems on plastic art, no less than in those on music, he shows a technical knowledge that is surprising.   But he has done more than this ; he traces, and makes his readers feel, a relation between the soul of man and the soul of music, and he interprets the effects of music on the emotions in words which have never been excelled.   It may be taken that he considered music as the highest art.

STYLE.—Coming to his technical achievements, we cannot fail to be impressed by Browning's remarkable power of rhyme as well as of variety in versification.   No poet more clearly shows the spirit by the metrical rhythm of the lines.   The mere arrangement of the words calls up a striking picture, so striking indeed that it could not be re-produced in painting or sculpture ; no art but the words themselves could bring the picture so vividly before us.   Browning excels most other poets in this power of word-painting.   As a rule, a good description of external objects is improved by a good illustration, or at least such illustration is possible ; but the artist would labour in vain who tried to depict on canvas the actual scene which Browning has described to us.   If any artist doubts the truth of this, let him try for himself to present the sky as described in *Easter Day*, the poet as portrayed in *How it Strikes a Contemporary*.   This power of allying sound with sense is very noticeable in *How they brought the Good News from Ghent to Aix*.   The words seem, as it were, tumbling over each other in the haste and excitement to reach a climax, and few can read the poem without feeling breathless at the end of it. Equally forcible is the calm and solemn atmosphere we breathe in *Evelyn Hope ;* the pathos of a child's death rather than awe at the death of an active worker.

Another, perhaps the most striking feature of Browning's work, is the robustness which characterises the matter of his poems, and which appears in an equally marked degree in their form. They present a noteworthy illustration of "mens sana in corpore sano." His clear, strong, energetic mind, unhampered by ill-health, seems to grasp the actual significance of man's life ; and his deep sympathy with all that is real in man enables him to transmit the feeling of reality to all his works. Throughout there is nothing morbid, nothing weak, and little that is vague. He not only seems thoroughly alive and vigorous himself, but he endows with actual life and vigour every character which he introduces.

His power of description is keen, but this, like everything else, is kept in subordination to the study of soul—the study which was the aim of Browning's life, and for the sake of which he chose poetry as his vocation. His capabilities would have fitted him equally well for a musician or a painter, but his choice fell once for all on poetry, as dealing more closely with human interests. In this study of the lives of men his vast sympathies led him to treat of innumerable varieties of periods, places, and people. Whether he deals with ancient, mediæval, or modern subjects, the liberality of moral range is as great as the variety of type ; and, belonging to a time when scientific research is far-reaching, keen, and critical as to the history of life, Browning is equally far-reaching, keen, and critical in his research for all the facts and details of the life of the soul. His wide scope of subject is invariably bound up with a wide extent of knowledge. He was in every sense a scholar, and his minute knowledge of animate and inanimate life add greatly to the vividness and force of his poetry.

OBSCURITY.—Before we turn to consider the poems in detail, another point arrests our attention. It is the ever-repeated charge of obscurity which the critical and uncritical alike bring against Browning. In some cases the charge must be admitted. At the same time the accusation is often brought by those who attempt to glance through his works as a mere relaxation and pastime. The full enjoyment, however, of Browning, as of Shakespeare, cannot be had without study, and the thinking powers of his readers are specially called into use by his poetry. Perhaps Browning cared too little for popularity. Believing, as he did, that only the motives of life are seriously of consequence, and again that every failure is but a step to success, he would not be discouraged. In a preface to *Strafford* (1837) he writes: "While a trifling success would much gratify, failure will not wholly discourage me from another effort: experience is to come, and earnest endeavour may yet remove many disadvantages." In a later preface, that to *Sordello* (1863), he acknowledges with commendable modesty such shortcomings as may have provoked hostile criticism. "My own faults of expression were many; but with care for a man or book such would be surmounted, and without it, what avails the faultlessness of either?" In his determination neither to sacrifice sense to sound, nor fact to form, and to use no superfluous words which might weaken the force of his meaning, Browning perhaps went to the other extreme, and acquired to excess the habit of condensation, of rugged and abrupt expression, and so defeated his own ends. But if this be occasionally true, it is nevertheless the exception rather than the rule. It is true that with the character-istic modesty before referred to, he often ignored the fact that his own intellect was superior to that of his readers. Realising that his own clear mind could retain the original thread of the subject, while he went off at a tangent, and devoted a page or two to some subordinate topic which he had touched on in passing, and which had started a new train of ideas, he forgot that his readers could not keep pace with such a digression. In this way his intel-lect sometimes not only renders him liable to the charge of obscurity, but substantially interferes with his dramatic effect. There is, however, very little of his poetry from which a second reading does not lift the veil that at first conceals from our eyes the beauty and the truth that it contains.

In reading passages in Browning which at first sight seem difficult, it is well to remember that apparently he makes a practice of setting down his thoughts almost in the precise words in which he thinks them. This means, not only that the reader must supply the minor words necessary to the strict expression of the thought, a task not difficult, if he remembers that he is free to do it, but also that he must put up with many phrases and con-structions which would not be habitual in a writer whose reading was less wide and less completely absorbed than Browning's was. A reader is also liable to try to read more into the lines than the plain sense ; and that is a very great mistake with Browning, who is seldom mystical. His wife well describes the spirit in which such works should be read :—

> " We get no good
> By being ungenerous, even to a book,
> And calculating profits,—so much help
> By so much reading.   It is rather when
> We gloriously forget ourselves and plunge
> Soul-forward, headlong, into a book's profound,
> Impassioned for its beauty and salt of truth—
> 'Tis then we get the right good from a book."

CHAPTER III.

THE POEMS.

Vol. I.—*Pauline*, 1833, written when the poet was only twenty, is a fragment of the confession of a poet to his lady-love. It serves as a sort of introduction to the characteristics of Browning's later work—notably his religious fervour, his knowledge of the Greek classics, his love of music and the Fine Arts, and his keen power of analysis of the human mind. It is also distinct from the other love poems, inasmuch as the lover's interest is centred in himself. *Pauline* is a monologue, utterly devoid of action, describing the various phases of a lover's mind. It is evident throughout his confession that Pauline's lover is a man with noble thoughts and a vast spiritual ambition, but without the energy necessary to the realisation of his longings. Immeasurably self-conscious and morbid, he has spent his time in dreaming of high ideals instead of labouring to attain them. From his self-accusations it seems as if morbid introspection had given place to a reaction of wild and evil behaviour, which included even temporary faithlessness to Pauline. His better nature, however, at last re-asserts itself and leads him back to Pauline, in whose never-failing love he at last finds peace.

14

The poem contains frequent reference to Browning's love
and admiration for Shelley, whom he idealises throughout
as the " Suntreader."

In *Sordello*, 1840, Browning has traced the development
of a poet's soul among the discordant elements of mediæval
Italy. The historical episodes serve as a mere background
to this study of soul. The Guelfs, the party supporting the
ascendancy of the Pope, struggle for supremacy with the
Ghibellines, who are led by the Emperor Frederick.
Sordello first appears as a dreamy youth living in the
castle of Goïto, under the protection of Ecelin Romano,
one of the chief leaders on the Emperor's side. All that
is known of Sordello's birth is, that he is reported to be
the child of a poor archer who had saved the life of
Ecelin's wife and child. Out of gratitude, Ecelin and his
wife, Adelaide of Este, have brought up the orphan,
Sordello. The years which he passes at Goïto have
brought forth great events in the world. Ecelin has
grown old and retired from active service, and his son is
not capable of replacing him. The chief burden of the
Ghibelline cause rests on Taurello Salinguerra, a brave
and chivalrous soldier who carries all before him. The
Guelfs are utterly routed, and great rejoicings take place
at Mantua. Hither comes Sordello to compete in song
with other troubadours. He is triumphant and is proclaimed poet to the Lady Palma of Este, daughter of
Ecelin, by his first wife, Agnes of Este. In Lady Palma
he sees his fate. His love is returned, but, unfortunately,
she is not free to choose, for her friends intend her to
marry Count Richard Bonifacio. He is a Guelf whom it
is very desirable to attach firmly to the Pope, while Sordello is nameless and a Ghibelline. But under Palma's
influence, Sordello's views undergo a change, and he

then becomes only anxious that the great soldier Taurello shall change with him from the Emperor's to the Pope's side.

While he is vainly endeavouring to achieve this, the discovery is made that Sordello is not the child of a poor archer, but of Taurello himself. The secret was known to Adelaide of Este, but she kept silence from fear of rivalry between Sordello and her own son, and she is now dead. Taurello rejoices that this famous poet should be no other than his son, and sets before him the grandest of careers, on condition that he shall reject his new Guelf ideas, and remain a Ghibelline. In the event of his consenting to this, Taurello promises that he shall marry Palma, and shall succeed to the command of the Ghibelline party. After long and earnest debate, in which temptation presses sorely, Sordello decides to yield to the dictates of his conscience, and to renounce all hope of Palma and happiness. But the severe mental strain has been too much for the fragile, sensitive poet, and when Taurello returns for his reply, bringing Palma with him, they find Sordello dead, and the badge, which would have proclaimed his future happiness and infidelity, trampled under foot. The rest of the poem dwells upon Taurello's later life and exploits.

Although *Sordello* is undoubtedly the most difficult of all Browning's works, it contains much that is well worth the careful study which is necessary to the comprehension of the whole. The digression in the third book, although it seems out of place there, coming as it does at the crisis of Sordello's life, is, nevertheless, interesting in itself as setting forth many important ideas and aims of Browning's work.

VOL. II.—*Paracelsus*, 1835, is an account sufficiently idealised for the purposes of poetry of the great doctor-quack of the sixteenth century. The details of his life are exactly followed, and side by side with these Browning has endeavoured to portray the probable inner life of the man, with his cleverness, his intolerance, and his ambition. The poem is divided into five scenes, each showing a crisis in Paracelsus' life. Three minor characters are introduced—Festus and his wife Michal to represent the simply human element; and Aprile, an Italian poet, who is a type of the power of Love, just as Paracelsus is a type of the power of Knowledge. Both are unregulated powers, neither complete without the other, and neither therefore realising success.

The first scene, *Paracelsus Aspires*, takes place at Würzburg on the eve of Paracelsus' departure from the home which, until then, he had shared with Festus and Michal. Both of these endeavour to dissuade him from the solitary path he has chosen, and this leads Paracelsus to explain and defend his aims. He believes it to be his mission to acquire knowledge—such knowledge as will benefit mankind, but he feels that he can only acquire it through hitherto untried methods, and at the sacrifice of human joys. Festus regards this as a delusion, and tries to combat it with arguments of common sense. Paracelsus, however, overrules them, and declares—

" I go to prove my soul !
I see my way as birds their trackless way.
I shall arrive ! what time, what circuit first,
I ask not : but unless God send his hail
Or blinding fire-balls, sleet or stifling snow,

B

In some time, his good time, I shall arrive :
He guides me and the bird.   In his good time !"

Festus answers that the path of knowledge is not trackless.   There are footprints left by the great men gone
before.   Nature has written her secrets, not in desert
places, but in the souls of men—such men as the
Stagirite,[1] and many more.   He urges Paracelsus to first
learn what they can teach, and then go farther on the
same path.   He warns him earnestly against personal
ambition which will corrupt his unselfish thirst for knowledge, against the presumption which will lead him to
serve God in other than the appointed way, and equally
against the dangers of a course which will cut him off
from human love.   But Paracelsus has his answer ready.
The wisdom of the past has done nothing for mankind.
Men have laboured and grown famous, but the evils of
earth are unabated.   Truth comes from within ourselves, and *to know* is to have opened a door to let truth
out, not to admit it.   The force which inspires him
proves that his mission comes from a higher power.
His own will could not create such promptings, and
he dares not set them aside.   The depth of his convictions carries the day, and the scene closes with the
avowal from both Festus and Michal, that they have
faith in him.

The second scene, *Paracelsus Attains*, takes place
nine years later, in the house of a Greek conjuror at Con-
stantinople.   Here we find Paracelsus reviewing his past
life and writing an account of it at the bidding of the

---

[1] Aristotle.

conjuror, by whose help he is now hoping to learn the
secret which these nine years have failed to teach him.
Even while he seeks such help, he realises how low he
has sunk since God's help no longer suffices him, and he
is willing to receive a mere conjuror's help instead.   As
he sits wrapped in thought, the idea flashes through
his brain that he may be going mad, and he prays long
and fervently against such punishment.   Ending this
prayer, he hears from within the voice of Aprile, an
Italian poet, singing a song of those who have failed
before, and who are lost.   With the last words of the
song, Aprile enters.   He is one of those who have failed,
and his fate unconsciously teaches Paracelsus one great
reason of his own failure.   Aprile relates how he has
loved and sought love with endless passion, caring for
nothing else.   He explains that his love included not
alone human love, but love of all things beautiful in Art
and Nature, and how he longed to give this beauty to
man.   But he feels at last how in striving after this he
has wasted his powers and his life, and has lived in utter
selfishness, because he has not tried to create any of this
beauty, but merely to possess it.   Now this vain remorse
comes too late.   The hand of death is heavy on him, and
almost with the last words of his confession, Aprile dies.
His story, however, has taught Paracelsus the lesson that
he must use his knowledge in love for men, and must
not neglect such immediate service to follow a vague
ideal passion.

The third scene, *Paracelsus*, occurs five years later at
Basle, where Festus has come to visit his friend for the
first time during the fourteen years which have passed
since he set out on his quest.   Paracelsus is now at the
height of his fame as a professor of medicine at Basle

Festus had been present at his lecture that morning, and had seen how largely it was attended, and he now enthusiastically tells Paracelsus how he glories in his success. Then Paracelsus owns the truth. His apparent success is mere outward show: inwardly, in his own heart, he has failed, for he is no nearer the truth than when he started; and, indeed, he has learnt to be content with lower aims. He is very bitter in his self-reproach, and it is now Festus's turn to encourage him: but Festus's very love only adds to the despair that overwhelms him, which he pathetically expresses thus—

> "No, no:
> Love, hope, fear, faith—these make humanity;
> These are its sign and note and character,
> And these I have lost!"

In the fourth scene, *Paracelsus Aspires* once more. It is two years since the night at Basle when he opened his heart to Festus, and he is now at Colmar. He has been driven ignominiously from Basle as an "egregious cheat," and he now sends for Festus, and tells him of that and of his future plans and aspirations. These aspirations have become very complex and hard to understand, and despite his somewhat softened manner it is evident that he has greatly deteriorated, and we cannot but feel that from this downward path there will be no return. Festus feels this too, but still he is more hopeful of Paracelsus' future, since he now seems nearer to human love, and this hope seems justified by the profoundly touching manner in which, on hearing of Michal's death, Paracelsus forgets his personal griefs to comfort Festus.

The last scene of all, *Paracelsus Attains,* takes place in the hospital at Salzburg, thirteen years later.

Paracelsus lies dying. His faithful Festus is watching beside him in love, grief, and prayer. Paracelsus is delirious, and dreams of the poet Aprile. He has heard Aprile all night singing in Paradise, and in his pardon Paracelsus feels his own. Wild words follow about his past life; then he dreams about Aprile and Michal together, and struggles to keep near to them and to love. Then, half-conscious, he prays for his old power, for full attainment of his aims, and for Divine approval; and as he realises that such things cannot be in this world, he feels absolute faith that there must be a world to come. Then his mind wanders again, but at last Festus succeeds in rousing him to full consciousness, and he then sums up the whole of his past life, and the lessons it should teach, in a wonderful, prophetic death-bed vision.

Apart from its strong psychological interest, this poem serves as a sort of index to Browning's ideas and faith more fully developed in his later work, and is in many parts eloquent and musical. The song, "Over the sea our galleys went," is one of the finest lyrics in the English language.

Strafford, 1837, an Historical Tragedy, as it is called, presents less interest from the historical than from the simply human point of view. The historical events of the time are for the most part merely referred to, and those which are actually set before us serve simply as so many pegs on which the poet chooses to hang the touching picture of Strafford's devotion to the person of the king. This devotion is the more remarkable because it is obvious that it is simply love for Charles, not sympathy with his cause, which actuates Strafford throughout. Browning

has entirely discarded the usual halo with which it is usual
to surround Charles I., and he appears before us as mean
and despicable a character as the Roundheads themselves
could have desired.   His treachery and vacillation, however, form a convenient foil to Strafford, with his perfect
loyalty which no amount of deceit nor the fear of death
can shake.   He is true to the end, and with his dying words
thanks God that, since Charles too must die, he is at least
spared the pain of outliving him.   Pym, with his passionate devotion to the ideal of England which he cherished, is
also an interesting character, more especially when his
love for his old friend Strafford struggles with and is
overthrown by his sense of duty to his country.   His farewell speech to Strafford, expressing the confident hope that
they will meet hereafter when Strafford's sin of desertion
shall have been pardoned, is very touching.   The imaginary
character of Lady Carlisle, with her silent love for Strafford,
whom she all but saves, is the picture of a true woman.

Vol. III.—*Pippa Passes*, 1841, although frequently included under the head of the dramas, is not entirely a
play, though it contains as true a dramatic spirit as anything Browning has written.   It consists of a series of
dramatic scenes connected by one central, poetical idea.
The idea is that of the unconscious influence which even
the humblest of God's creatures may exercise over the lives
around it.   Incidentally it shows how impossible it is for
one human being to estimate the actual life and happiness
of a fellow-creature.   The simple picture of the happy
little silk-girl, Pippa, who, by her singing, unconsciously
carries God's message to the hearts of those she supposed
the happiest in Asolo, is in exquisite relief to the per-
plexities depicted in the four principal scenes.   The

first of these shows us Ottima, who has murdered her husband that she may the more freely enjoy the guilty love of Sebald, her confederate in the crime. Her paramour, however, now that the deed is done, lacks courage to enjoy the fruits of it. Ottima, on the contrary, gloats over and glories in her crime, and has almost succeeded in silencing Sebald's remorse, when Pippa passes singing. Her song, with its simple refrain,

> " God's in his heaven—
> All's right with the world,"

awakens his almost sleeping conscience. He heaps reproaches and abuse on his accomplice, and in an access of remorse and despair kills himself, while Ottima bursts forth into a cry of passionate and unchanged love for him. In this one scene is concentrated a whole tragedy of the most powerful kind. A few lines depict with startling vividness the two characters —Ottima, strong, passionate, and determined, and Sebald, weak, vacillating, and remorseful. Pippa passes on, and we come to an Interlude, which serves as a connecting link with the rest of the poem. This is the "Talk by the Way" of a group of students who have played a practical joke on their comrade, Jules, by which he is made to believe that he has married a lady of birth who has admired his work. In the episode following, Jules has just returned with his bride from the church ; in reply to his endearing words she recites to him scoffing verses dictated to her by his jealous fellow-students, from which he learns the truth that his wife is only a sculptor's model and the creature of an infamous woman. While his anger is at its height he hears the voice of Pippa singing on her way; his heart is filled with pity for his wife, Phene, who loves him so well, and he determines that he will take her far away from all who knew them here, and that henceforward he will live for her and Art alone. Special interest attaches to this scene because it contains one of the earliest of Browning's dissertations upon Art. Pippa next passes the house of Luigi, a young patriot, whose mother is trying to dissuade him from the murder of the Austrian tyrant. Just as she seems about to gain her point, Pippa passes, and her song so rouses Luigi's latent patriotism that he starts on his mission at once, and thus escapes being arrested.

Last of all, Pippa passes by the Bishop's palace while he is discussing a plan with his Intendant by which they can make away with Pippa, who, we now learn, is the daughter of the Bishop's dead brother, at whose murder both the Bishop and his Intendant had connived. As the sound of Pippa's song reaches them, the Bishop's better self prevails and he orders the Intendant's arrest.

All unconscious of the wonders she has wrought, Pippa returns home still singing, and wondering vaguely whether it could ever be possible that her life should in any way influence the lives of the great people about whom she has been dreaming all day.

King Victor and King Charles, 1842, is an historical tragedy based on the abdication of King Victor the Second, first king of Sardinia, in favour of his son Charles, for whom he had previously shown no affection whatever. His probable motive for abdication Browning assumes to have been the desire to bring about certain projects unpopular to the nation. His son, he imagined, would naturally defer to the father who so nobly yielded up the crown to him, and thus he would be able to execute his desires while he escaped the ill-favour which would ensue from them. Charles, however, in great measure owing to Polyxena his wife, was less compliant than his father wished. A year after his abdication, Victor, finding that his schemes have not so progressed, returns to demand the restitution of his crown. It appears to Charles, however, that such restitution now would be mere desertion of his post, for the improvements throughout the land since his rule began are very obvious. He therefore refuses, and Victor at once sets about raising an army to recover his crown by force. By the vigilance of the minister d'Ormea, however, he is arrested and brought back to Charles as a prisoner. Horror at the idea of keeping his father captive induces Charles to condemn d'Ormea's interference, and to acknowledge Victor as king. This proves, however, to be a mere matter of form, for it is soon evident that Victor is a dying man. His death, immediately after his re-installation to the throne, is the only point in the play which is not absolutely historical. In reality he survived a year in a state of semi-insanity. Polyxena is a fine study of a strong, right-minded woman, clear-sighted through her great love, and thus able to see alike through Victor's wiles and the time-serving devotion of d'Ormea, and so to help her husband to withstand them.

The Return of the Druses, 1843, is a tragedy in five acts, enveloped in the romance and mystery of the East. The scene is laid in the fifteenth century, in an island of the South Sporades, inhabited by Druses of Lebanon, and garrisoned by the Knights-Hospitallers of Rhodes. The plot is elaborate for Browning, and throughout the tragedy there runs an intense active excitement which is highly dramatic. The play turns on the passionate desire of a Druse chief, Djabal, to free his nation from the tyranny of the Christian Prefect under which they groan. But the people fear that resistance will only provoke worse treatment, and they believe that deliverance can only be achieved by the return to earth of a Druse divinity, Hakeem. Djabal has overheard Anael, a maiden of the tribe, declare that she will love only one who saves her people, and partly in order to gain her love, and almost in self-deception, he has proclaimed himself Hakeem. He has been received with implicit faith, and the action of the play takes place on the very day on which he stands pledged to slay the Prefect, to exalt himself, and to appear before the tribe no longer Djabal, but Hakeem. Anael alone secretly doubts his divinity, and, overwhelmed with shame at such doubt, she resolves that she will herself slay the Prefect, and thus prove to herself not less than to Djabal (who, as Hakeem, must already know her unworthiness) her restored faith in him. Had they but known, help was already at hand without need of murder. Loys, a Christian knight-novice, whom Djabal had sent to Rhodes for safety from the massacre which was imminent, had used his absence to such purpose, that he returned that day to announce the deposition of the tyrant Prefect, whose place he was more worthily to fill. The state of excitement in which he found the isle induced him to delay his news until the Pope's Nuncio should arrive and formally instal him. Ignorant of this, however, Anael slays the Prefect, and when Djabal comes prepared to do the deed himself, he finds no Prefect, but Anael, pale and trembling, with a blood-stained dagger in her hands. Horror-stricken at the result of his deception, Djabal reveals his imposture to her. Anael, incredulous at first, slowly grasps the truth, and, while retaining her love for him, urges his confession to the tribe. He refuses, and with a passionate outburst of scorn she leaves him, seeks the Nuncio, and denounces Djabal as an impostor. The Nuncio uses Anael's accusation, to which he adds the charge of the Prefect's murder, to try and weaken Djabal's influence with the Druses, for he fears that, being a Christian and delegate of the Church, he may also share and suffer from the hatred against the late Prefect. His eloquence is such that the Druses seem to waver in their allegiance, and the Nuncio at once orders Djabal to be brought before them, and repeats his accusations to his face. Djabal challenges him to name one Druse who accuses him, and Anael is brought in veiled. No one recognises her, and the veil is indignantly torn from her by Khalil, her brother and Djabal's most faithful adherent. When he sees who his accuser is, Djabal, bowed with shame and remorse, yet feeling that his punishment is just, calls upon Anael to pronounce his doom. But the full tide of her love returns upon Anael. She utters one cry, the acclamation "Hakeem!" and falls dead at his feet. The Druses think that his wrath has killed her, and at once fall down in worship. At the same moment the sound is heard of the trumpet announcing help from Venice. Thus assured of the speedy deliverance of his people, Djabal stabs himself over Anael's body, and so, through her sacrifice of truth to love, he remains for ever Hakeem to the Druses.

It is frequently alleged that Browning has not sufficiently accounted for Anael's death, but it is a well-known fact that people have died ere now from the effect of a great shock, and it seems scarcely strange that the horror of a pure-minded and hitherto innocent girl at suddenly finding herself transformed into a murderess, the grief and shame at her lover's imposture, and the supreme effort by which she herself supported it, should combine to kill her.

A Soul's Tragedy (1846).—In this, as the title suggests, the inner drama presents the greatest interest, although it is set in a background of distinctly interesting action. The first act, "being the poetry of Chiappino's life," shows his apparent nobleness and devotion to his friend Luitolfo, who, in anger at the unjust sentence of exile which had been passed on Chiappino, has stabbed and he believes murdered the Provost. Luitolfo, dazed with terror, and thinking that the Provost's guards are after him, accepts Chiappino's offer of escape and leaves him to meet the guards. The next moment proves that it is a crowd of the populace who are approaching ; the murder has acted as a signal for revolt, and with cheers and joy the people come to hail the murderer as their saviour. Chiappino accepts the position without a thought, though honour requires him to disclose that Luitolfo, and not he, had done the deed. In this begins the tragedy of the ruin of his soul. The second part, "being the prose of Chiappino's life," shows the further deterioration of his moral character, and ends with his exposure by the Pope's Legate, who leads him on, with the hope of being made Provost himself, to change his politics and principles, and abandon the duties of friendship. Having made him reveal his own baseness, the Legate proceeds to hold him up to the scorn which he deserves, and finally completes his discomfiture by announcing that the Provost had not been killed but only wounded. Luitolfo is therefore able to return to the city, which Chiappino as promptly leaves.

The prose is admirably written, and is as forcible and concise as the poetry.

Vol. IV.—*A Blot on the 'Scutcheon* (1843), the simplest of all the plays, is at once the most pathetic and most human. Every gentle feeling of love and pity is awakened for the child-like, tender Mildred Tresham, who drifted into sin almost from very innocence, and whose one heart-rending cry is, "I had no mother, God forgot me, and I fell;"—while reverence deep and true is aroused for Guendolen, Mildred's cousin and true friend, who in the early scenes furnishes the brightness and gaiety of the play, but who in time of trouble proves the depth of her love and loyalty. The character of Mildred's lover, Lord Henry Mertoun, presents a touching sketch of boyish weakness and devoted love, on the verge of developing into manly resolution. The central figure of the play is, however, Thorold, Lord Tresham, with his overweening pride in the honour of his house, tempered only by a passionate love for the sister to whom he has stood for both father and mother. Unspeakably touching is the scene in the second act, where, after first dwelling long and tenderly on "a brother's love for a sole sister," he urges Mildred to confess her guilty love, promising that he will help her, that she shall marry her lover, and that somehow they two "will wear this day out." Then follows, in powerful contrast, the revulsion of feeling at what seems her utter depravity in refusing either to name her lover, or to forbid the advances of Lord Henry Mertoun, which facts even Thorold's love is not keen enough to connect. Maddened at her apparent double sin, he curses Mildred, and then with rash haste surprises Mertoun under Mildred's window, and kills him. Then, too late, he realises the truth, and, feeling that the wrong he has committed through want of thought can only be expiated by his sharing Mildred's and Mertoun's fate, he takes poison.　Mildred dies broken-hearted in his arms a few minutes before his death, but the eyes of brother and sister see clearly now, and in their mutual forgiveness death re-unites them.　The tragic interest of the play is greatly heightened by the fact that Guendolen discovers the truth only just too late to save the lives of all three.　The language throughout is poetical and beautiful in the extreme, the love-song in the first act being one of the most charming and melodious of Browning's lyrics.

Colombe's Birthday, 1844, is an imaginary historical play turning on the question of the Salic law.　The chief interest, however, lies less in this than in the internal drama which centres in Colombe, the supposed Duchess of Cleves, who in one day passes through almost every phase of human emotion, and who at last emerges strong and triumphant from the struggle, having yielded up the prospect of becoming empress, because she felt that "love, not vanity, is best."　Surrounding Colombe are the characters of the nobles of her court, the rival claimant to her Duchy, his confidant, Melchior, and Valence, the advocate of Cleves, whose loyalty and courage carry the day and win her love.　Each of these, with scarcely an exception, is a finished picture imbued with a distinct personality.

MEN AND WOMEN (1855).—The title of this collection is admirably significant of the variety of subject and style which we may expect to find in it.　Criticism, argument, painting, religion, mythology, and love alike have place here, and vie with each other in subtlety of thought and beauty of expression.

Transcendentalism, a poem in twelve books, is evidently an imaginary title quoted in order to address to an imaginary author words of criticism and encouragement. The fault lies, his critic says, in that the youthful poet speaks his thoughts instead of singing them. He has also fallen into the error of thinking that only youth needs "images and melody" whereas, in reality, age needs them most, and finds more comfort in what throws a halo of glory over the commonplace than in philosophy or intricate thought.

How it Strikes a Contemporary expresses a humorous, almost contemptuous criticism upon the slight value which should be placed on popular opinion. The subject of the poem is a Spanish poet, whose characteristic dress and manner arouse suspicion that he is a spy. A graphic description of the wealth which he is supposed to enjoy forms a dramatic contrast to the picture of the garret in which he dies.

Artemis Prologizes was originally intended for a poem of some length, but was unfortunately never completed. It takes up the story of Hippolytus, as told by Euripides, and continues where he left off. According to Euripides, Hippolytus, son of Hippolyta and Theseus, offended Venus by his aversion to women and by his worship of the godess Artemis. Hippolyta died, and Theseus then married Phaedra, daughter of Minos, king of Crete. To revenge herself on Hippolytus, Venus caused Phaedra to fall in love with her step-son. He repulsed her love, and Phaedra killed herself, but left a letter accusing Hippolytus of guilty love for her. Theseus, enraged, sought no explanation of his son, but prayed for vengeance on him from Neptune, who had promised Theseus to grant him three requests. Accordingly, as Hippolytus was driving his chariot along the coast, Neptune sent a bull out from the sea. The horses were frightened, upset the chariot, and Hippolytus was mortally wounded. As he was dying, Artemis appeared to him, and told him that such a death was his fate. This ends the tragedy as told by Euripides. Browning continues the story in a monologue descriptive of all that has occurred since Phaedra's confession down to the actual time of the poem, when Artemis, assisted by Aesculapius, is nursing the still unconscious Hippolytus back to life.

An Epistle containing the *Strange Medical Experience of Karshish, the Arab Physician*, gives an account of the raising of Lazarus from an entirely new point of view. Karshish writes to the imaginary sage, Abib, about a man named Lazarus who was seized with an epileptic fit, from which he was roused too soon, the result being that his reason is affected. Karshish explains that Lazarus regards his recovery from the fit as a Divine miracle, and that he asserts the Nazarene physician who attended him was God Himself. Karshish repeats that he well knows this is merely madness, but yet the strangeness of the idea and the consistency of Lazarus' story puzzle him sorely, and he cannot forget it. He therefore seeks Abib's opinion on the matter.

Johannes Agricola is an imaginary soliloquy of the German of that name, who in the sixteenth century founded the sect of the Antinomians. The tenets of their faith denied the power of freewill for good or evil, but maintained that some human beings were elect, and therefore could do no wrong, sin as they might, while the good attempted by others was doomed to turn to evil. Johannes Agricola wonders at such a state of things, but accepts it, and feels only gratitude that God is entirely incomprehensible, since it places His love beyond all price.

Pictor Ignotus is the lament of an unknown painter, who hears praise lavished upon a rival. He too, he says, could have become famous, but to achieve this, his pictures must have been sold, and he preferred to die unhonoured and unknown rather than that the pictures he deemed so sacred should become mere matter of merchandise and trade. The speaker feels assured that the consciousness of such dishonour would have utterly cancelled the delights of fame; but there is, nevertheless, a vein of intense and bitter longing for glory, which he admits would have been bought too dear.

Fra Lippo Lippi possesses a double interest both as a transcript from life, and also as setting forth in definite terms our poet's view of one of the great services and the true aim of Art. In a delightfully humorous and witty monologue Fra Lippo Lippi relates to the Watch, who have just arrested him at midnight in a suspicious neighbourhood, the story and reason of his escapade. His patron, Cosmo dei Medici, had locked him in a room of the palace, that he might the sooner complete some pictures on which he was at work. Fra Lippo Lippi, however, found this imprisonment unbearable. In the street below he caught the sound of voices singing, and heard the patter of feet. Looking out of the window he caught a glimpse of a pretty face; then, without further effort at self-control, he tore his bedclothes into strips, made a rope of them and dropped down into the street below. His frolic over, he was returning home when he was arrested. On his way back he entertains his captors with an account of his life, telling them how he was lured into a convent at the age of eight, when he was starving, and would have sold his soul for bread; how he had a talent for drawing, of which the Carmelites made use,

C

but the full development of which they stunted by their
narrow-minded prejudices. The monks found his painting too fleshly, because it represented Nature, and, they
declared, did not stimulate devotion.   But, urges Fra
Lippo Lippi, a bell can call folks to matins and vespers,
but it cannot inspire devotion ; it is the province of Art
to convey to them

> " The beauty and the wonder and the power,
> The shapes of things, their colours, lights and shades,
> Changes, surprises,—and God made it all ! "

It may be urged, he admits, that since it is God's
world, what need is there that man should strive to re-
produce it ? He answers

> " For, don't you mark ?   We're made so that we love
> First when we see them painted, things we have passed
> Perhaps a hundred times nor cared to see ;
> And so they are better, painted—better to us,
> Which is the same thing.   Art was given for that."

Andrea del Sarto gives a pathetic picture of energy
and power wasted and misdirected through the love and
evil influence of a beautiful but worthless woman.   Conscious as he still is of the potentialities his soul might
have realised, Andrea del Sarto remains the willing slave
of a heartless wife, who, for the sake of her guilty love,
despises the sacrifice of his life and genius.   He now feels
that his mind has lost its power, though his hand retains
its cunning.

> " A man's reach should exceed his grasp,
> Or what's a heaven for ? "

The Bishop Orders His Tomb at St. Fraxed's Church is a typical study of the Renaissance, and of its influence upon man and Art. The Bishop is dying, and his last moments are spent not in regret for a life which, by his own confession, has been sensuous and worldly, but in giving elaborate instructions about his tomb. The minute details of the costly marbles, the bronze frieze, the ball of lapis-lazuli, *et cetera*, with which he desires it to be decorated, make it very evident what a wide knowledge of art and sculpture the Bishop possessed, and how high was his regard for these ; but it is also clear that the love of the beautiful is in no way allied with spiritual emotion. His so-called nephews, whom he now first acknowledges as his sons, are round his deathbed, and he implores them, with a fervour worthy of a better cause, to carry out his wishes, the chief of which is that they shall cast into insignificance the humbler tomb of a detested rival now lying in the same church.

Bishop Blougram's Apology is in reality a dialogue, although it is written in Browning's favourite form of monologue. Bishop Blougram,[1] a Roman Catholic priest, has invited to dinner a young literary man, Mr. Gigadibs, who is a professed free-thinker. Like all such, he is very anxious to air his views and to convince the Bishop of the folly of his episcopal ways. Coming straight to the point, Gigadibs after dinner hazards the opinion that the Bishop must see through the absurdity of the views he professes to hold and teach, and that he thus places himself in a false position. Gigadibs asserts that even he is more true and sincere than the

---

1 Supposed to be taken from Cardinal Wiseman. Cf. Chap. II. page 6.

Bishop, because he boldly states his unbelief, while the
Bishop is a disbeliever, but has not the courage to own
his convictions.   Hence, from adhering to a faith in
which he does not believe, Bishop Blougram loses the
sense of the ideal life which Gigadibs considers a necessity.   The Bishop's reply, or as it is termed, "apology,"
is ingenious in the extreme, and is apparently successful
in the case of Gigadibs.   It must, however, strike the
reader that a great many of the arguments are simply
ironical, and are uttered in contempt for so shallow
a creature as Gigadibs, to whom Bishop Blougram
scorns to reveal the hidden noble depths of his soul,
which we feel must exist.   The poem is in blank
verse, and flows with vigour and ease, while apart
from its psychological interest it contains passages
of very great beauty, the more striking because of
the calm, argumentative atmosphere which surrounds
them.

Cleon is a study of Greek life and thought in the early
days of Christianity.   The poem is in the form of a letter
from Cleon the aged poet, in answer to one from Protus
the king, asking in what spirit Cleon is prepared for
death, which Protus feels cannot be far distant from
either of them.   He has suggested that, leaving work
behind him which will live and influence the world,
Cleon must be prepared to welcome death with less
regret than others less worthy.   Cleon denies this, declaring there is little pleasure in knowing that his works
will live, since he will not be there to enjoy the glory.
He then speaks of the possibility of a future life which
the doctrine of Christ has recently promulgated, and
with bitter longing he expresses his wish that he could
believe in

> " Some future state revealed to us by Zeus,
> Unlimited in capability
> For joy, as this is in desire for joy."

He cannot, however, grasp any other idea of God than Zeus and the philosophy which forms part of his worship, and, therefore, he rejects the idea of an after-life, since it has not been revealed by Zeus. As to St. Paul, who had recently been preaching in the neighbourhood, and of whom Protus asks for information, Cleon indignantly scorns the idea that—

> " .   .   .   a mere barbarian Jew
> .   .   .   .
> Hath access to a secret shut from us ? "

Apart from the religious motive of the poem, it is interesting for the remarkable picture it presents of Greek life in those days—the reverence for knowledge and wisdom, the love of Art, the incessant pursuit of pleasure, and, underlying all, the sense of incompletion or even despair at the thought that this world ends all.

Rudel to the Lady of Tripoli is a dainty little love-poem in which the French troubadour Rudel relates the legend of how the sun-flower acquired its name. To this flower he compares himself and his chivalrous passion for the unknown Lady of Tripoli, towards whom his life sets as the sun-flower turns ever to the sun.

One Word More. To E. B. B.—The exquisite tenderness and beauty of this sacred dedication to Mrs. Browning cannot be expressed in words. It needs no interpreter but the heart, and it is above criticism and beyond praise.

V. DRAMATIC ROMANCES (1845).—*Incident of the French Camp* is a stirring record of the patriotic loyalty of a soldier under Napoleon. The boy of Browning's poem was in reality a man, but in all other respects the story is true. Dying of wounds received while planting the flag over the market-place at Ratisbon, the soldier, nevertheless, succeeds in reaching the Emperor and in gasping out the good news. Napoleon gently says, "You're wounded." With a proud smile he answers, "I'm killed, sire," and falls dead.

The Patriot: an Old Story, illustrates the ingratitude which is the reward of unsuccessful devotion. Ignominious death awaits the hero of a year before; but faith is strong in him, and from God he hopefully looks for the reward denied him by men.

My Last Duchess is a perfect sketch of the noble of the Renaissance with his haughty pride of a "nine-hundred-years' old name," his jealousy untouched by love, his arrogation of sole homage and submission from all who come under his tyrannical sway. His late wife did not sufficiently appreciate the honour and splendour of her position : she lavished her smiles too freely on all around. The duke remonstrated with such effect that "all smiles stopped together," and the lady sank under the chilling, cheerless atmosphere, and died. The duke cannot regret his conduct. He feels that it was right, and he is now about to take another wife. While with protestations of his desire for herself he is negociating with an ambassador about her dowry, he relates his late wife's story, and, among other works of art, points out her picture. There is an apparent carelessness about the manner of the poem which is, however, calculated to set off to better advantage the significance of every detail.

Count Gismond turns on the mediæval faith in duel as arbiter in a cause of honour. Through the envy of two rivals, a girl is falsely accused of being unfit to hold the place of honour as queen of a certain tournament. As the calumny is spoken, a champion, Count Gismond, rises in her defence. He fights and kills her accuser, and leads the girl away to a happy future as his wife. The poem shows us the girl many years later, when she is relating to a friend the story of her deliverance.

The Boy and the Angel teaches the lesson of content in whatsoever place God has chosen to assign to each of us. The result of discontent is forcibly and eloquently set forth in the story of a boy, Theocrite, who longed to be Pope in order that he might the better praise God. The wish was granted, but God missed the humble praise from the boy, and sent the angel Gabriel to take his place. To no purpose. The place was Theocrite's, and none but he could fill it. So at last the angel sought the boy in his pomp as Pope, and showed him how he was out of place there, while his craftsman's cell was empty, his work there undone, and God unpraised. Theocrite saw the truth, and returned to his former station : a new Pope ruled at Rome, and when death came to each, "they sought God side by side."

Instans Tyrannus is a tribute to the power of conscience. A king confesses his unreasonable, inveterate hatred of one of his meaner subjects. His constant wish, to accomplish which he left no means of tyranny or temptation untried, was that the man should do some

wrong, which would justify the king in destroying him.
Enraged at the failure of every attempt to entrap him,
the king at last determined to crush him without any just
cause ; but at the crisis, just as the impending ruin was
at hand,

> " The man sprang to his feet,
>   Stood erect, caught at God's skirts, and prayed ! "

The tyrant stood terrified and abashed.

Mesmerism describes the experience of a man who
possesses the mesmeric power so strongly that when
separated from the woman he loves, he can nevertheless
so influence her, that, despite all hindrance, she is irresistibly compelled to come to him. The poem is less
interesting as a story than as a marvel of versification.
The breathless excitement of the speaker is perfectly reproduced in the breathless rush of the verse, in which a
minimum of punctuation makes the absolute intelligibi-
lity of the poem the more remarkable.

The Glove is a record of an old friend with a new
face. The story of the lady who tested her lover's
courage by flinging her glove among the lions, and thereby lost her lover and the king's favour, is familiar to
everyone. Browning, however, upholds the lady's conduct, and defends it on the plea that De Lorge was
always boasting of his courage, and never took any opportunity of proving it. The poem ends with a new and
original sequel in the lady's happy marriage with an
admiring witness, and De Lorge's less fortunate fate in
wedding a court beauty who was a favourite of the
king.

Time's Revenges.—A man soliloquises on a certain friend whose devotion and love are immeasurable, and whom he in return simply tolerates. His thoughts then turn to the lady he loves, and for whose sake he exults in killing "body and soul, and peace and fame," but who in her turn would calmly see him roasted alive, if so she could obtain a certain invitation which she longs for.

The Italian in England is interesting and affecting from its simplicity of manner and matter. The Italian, now an exile in England, relates the story of his escape through the courage and loyalty of a peasant girl, to whom in the desperation of hunger he revealed himself.

The Englishman in Italy presents a vastly different picture. It is written in brisk, animated verse, and is purely a descriptive poem consisting of a vivid picture of Italian peasant life, and of Italian scenery. The Englishman has taken refuge from the "scirocco" and rainstorm which had broken out, and he is whiling away the time by comforting and amusing a little frightened peasant girl with his cheery talk about all he had noticed of the national life and habits while the storm was still brewing. While he is speaking the sun shines out again, and the "scirocco" is gone—more quickly, he fears, than the political "scirocco" now overshadowing England.

In a Gondola is a love poem, marvellous in its subdued passion and power. The scene is an Italian lake, on which the lovers float by night, safe as they fondly hope from the jealous vigilance of "the three" who guard the lady. The sense of possible danger only adds to the intensity of their enjoyment and their love. Safely and happily they reach the lady's home, and the arrangements for the next night's meeting are completed, when the lover is surprised and stabbed. The glow of happiness which he has just experienced is with him still, and now will never leave him. So he dies content, having "lived indeed."

Waring is a sketch from life, and the hero was a personal friend of Browning's, Mr. Alfred Domett. He is represented in the poem as a man of great promise, but whose achievements always fell short of his possibilities, and who consequently remained unappreciated even by his friends. This lack of appreciation wounded his too sensitive nature, and he suddenly vanished from among his companions. In the first part of the poem, one of a group of friends is deploring Waring's sudden departure, and suggests all kinds of conjectures as to his whereabouts. The second part is spoken by one hitherto silent, but who now abruptly begins, "When I last saw Waring," and to the amazement of the rest he goes on to relate a meeting near Trieste, where he had seen Waring as the captain of a smuggling vessel.

The Twins, "Date" and "Dabitur," "Give" and "It shall be given unto you," relates the fable from Luther's "Table-Talk" how the success of Dabitur depends upon Date's well-being.

De Gustibus is one of the few poems in which Browning seems to have written about scenery for its own sake only. It contains no human interest whatever, but simply describes a couple of landscapes of English and Italian scenery.

A Light Woman.—The speaker has endeavoured to free his friend from the toils of such a woman. He has succeeded but too well, for he finds that he has gained the woman's heart himself at the cost of his friend's friendship. He has no love to give her, and when he reflects on the part he must seem to his friend to have played, he wonders which of the three is the most to be pitied.

The Last Ride Together has justly been called one of the finest lyrics of the century. It is charmingly melodious and full of subdued passion which, however, never drifts into sickly sentimentality. The rejected lover to whom the privilege of this last ride has been granted is throughout manly and noble. He realises that his failure is but one among many, and, as he muses on universal failure, he decides that it is best to lose bliss here and perchance gain it hereafter. Then as they ride on and on in silence his fancy suggests

> " What if . . . . . .
>   . . heaven just prove that I and she
> Ride, ride together, for ever ride."

The Pied Piper of Hamelin, written for and inscribed to the little son of Macready, the actor, is probably the best known of all Browning's shorter poems. The legend is familiar to all of the mysterious piper, who, by the irresistible and magnetic force of his music, cleared Hamelin of the rats with which the town was infested, and afterwards revenged himself for the non-payment of the stipulated fee by playing a still sweeter melody to draw the children after him out of the town. The poem has a singular simplicity and directness of style.

The Flight of the Duchess is probably entirely imaginary, although it reads like an old legend. It is said to have originated through one line of a song which Browning, when a boy, heard a gipsy sing on Guy Fawkes' Day, and which ran—

"Following the Queen of the Gipsies, oh !"

The story is told by an old huntsman thirty years after the flight of the Duchess, in whose escape he had assisted. The somewhat abrupt manner of the verse suggests admirably the good-hearted but rough and ready retainer, while the change to the mystic wonder and solemnity of the gipsy's song, revealing to the Duchess her gipsy origin, wakes an interest and an excitement throughout, which are perfectly delightful.

A Grammarian's Funeral describes the burial by his disciples of a man whose love has been devoted to study at the cost of everything else. They are carrying him to the topmost peak of a mountain, as a symbol of the noble heights to which he aspired. Uninteresting as the subject of a mere dry pedant may appear, Browning has dived into the heart and soul of the man and has portrayed with such masterly skill the spirit striving after what appeared to him the highest aim, that the old grammarian ceases to be dull and insignificant.

> "That low man seeks a little thing to do,
>   Sees it and does it :
>   This high man, with a great thing to pursue,
>   Dies ere he knows it."

The Heretic's Tragedy: A Middle-Age Interlude.— The victim of this tragedy is supposed to be Jacques du Bourg-Molay, who was burned at Paris A.D. 1314. The scene opens with an admonition from the Abbot expressing the infinite justice of God, notwithstanding his mercy. The chorus repeats the last line of the Abbot's sermon, "As infinite a justice too," with gruesome and indescribably powerful effect. The rest of the Interlude is sung by one person, the chorus again taking up the last line of every verse. The description of the stake and the agony of the victim are only the more keenly apparent through the grim humour of the language and the quaint formalities of the Interlude.

Holy-Cross Day.—In this poem also the language is for the first half grotesque and humorous, although it is not hard to find a serious and even tragic under-current in the irony with which the speaker describes the scene at Church, where on Holy-Cross Day (Sept. 14) at Rome a sermon was preached at which the attendance of the Jews was enforced. At the twelfth verse, however, this grim irony ceases, and there follows the magnificent and solemn death-song of Rabbi Ben Ezra. This prayer, at once a protest and a prophecy, defends the alleged conduct of the Jews, and ends with a triumphant expression of faith in God and confidence in the future.

Protus, an extract from an imaginary record, contains the history of how John the Pannonian, the blacksmith's son, usurped the crown of Protus, a tiny child of exceeding beauty, as to whose ultimate fate rumour varies. The poem begins with a description of a bust of Protus—

"   .   .   .   A baby face, with violets there,

  .   .   .   .   .   .
As those were all the little locks could bear."

The last lines describe a bust of the usurper, John, and form a striking example of Browning's power of expressing sense by sound.

The Statue and the Bust is more or less founded upon fact. In it Browning vigorously denounces the weakness of indecision and vacillation, and urges that, whatsoever man findeth to do, he should do it with his might. And this is what the hero and heroine of the *Statue and the Bust* did not do. The lady was married, but loved the Grand-Duke Frederick the First, who returned her love. They agreed to fly together, but, day after day, not from moral compunction but from mere infirmity of purpose, postponed their flight, until at last youth had passed and love had cooled, and only the memory of the past was left them. To ensure that this, at least, should live forever, the Duke caused an equestrian statue of himself riding away from the palace, but with his head turned towards the lady's window, to be erected in the square opposite ; while the lady ordered a bust of herself to be placed in the window, where she had daily watched for the Duke.

Porphyria's Lover[1] is a monologue spoken by a man who has murdered the woman he loves, but has no right to love. Yielding to momentary passion, she has come to him and confessed her love. In that supreme moment of happiness he felt that she was his "perfectly pure and good," and, that she may remain so for ever, he has murdered her. The matter-of-fact description, first of the weather, and then of the whole episode of the murder, add to the weird horror of the poem, which reveals marvellous dramatic power and concentration.

Childe Rolande to the Dark Tower Came is a strange, fantastic mixture of romance and realism. Romance

---

[1] Originally published with *Johannes Agricola* under the title of *Madhouse Cells.*

pure and simple is the legend of the knight who sets out in quest of the "Dark Tower," and who meets with none of the adventures common to the knights of old. Instead, he passes through a country barren and desolate, over which an awful silence reigns, a country so gloomy and a silence so hideous that imagination conjures up endless varieties of impossible horrors, while the vivid description of the terror of the place lends a ghastly realism to the fearful and wonderful scene. Undaunted by the overwhelming depression of his journey, Childe Rolande trudges bravely on, and at last meets with the success which had been denied to his predecessors. The poem is not an allegory, as is frequently suggested. The idea of it was first suggested by the line in "King Lear," which forms the title of the poem ; then, as Mrs. Orr tells us, a certain tower which struck Browning's poetic fancy led to the development of the idea, and the figure of a horse on some tapestry in his own drawing-room still further developed it, until it reached its present form.

Christmas Eve and Easter Day, 1850.—These poems are in no way sequels of each other. They are always classed together because they were published together, and both deal with the details of the Christian religion, and describe a vision of Christ. In *Christmas Eve* the speaker relates how the weather drove him for shelter into a small dissenting chapel on the borders of a common. But the preacher with his narrow-minded rant was more unpleasing to him than the wind and rain outside, and he left the chapel in hot haste. Once again outside in the storm, he began to think more tolerantly of what he had heard within. As he stood there meditating, the aspect of the sky suddenly

changed. The rain ceased, and a wonderful double
lunar rainbow shone across the heavens, and the Christ
in person stood before him. The face was turned from
him, but he caught the hem of the garment, and, so
holding, was borne in a vision to St. Peter's at Rome.
Without entering the cathedral he watched the whole cere-
mony; and, as he watched, he realised that faith and love
existed in the Roman Catholic worship which he was wit-
nessing, although in a different form from that in which
he had heretofore recognised it. The vision bore him
yet further, until they reached a lecture-hall in Germany,
where a freethinker was logically tracing the source of
the myth called Christianity. The lecturer's logic destroyed all idea of divinity, but attached almost equal
value to Christ's work as a man, because it led to God,
and to love, God's attribute. So here, too, the listener
found the basis of faith and love, though again differ-
ently expressed; and he felt that henceforth he would
not despise faiths alien to his own, but would believe
that before God they were as one. Such tolerance, however, was too near akin to indifference, and he suddenly
felt that he had lost even the hem of the garment, and
was again left to the mercy of the storm, which had re-
commenced. As the divine figure began to fade from
his sight, he realised his fault, and, once more catching
at the robe, held it until he found himself safe inside the
little chapel again, which, indeed, he seemed never to
have left. And then at last he had learnt the lesson not
to despise the lowliest form of love and faith, nor to
reject the truth in whatever form it might appear. The
second poem, *Easter Day*, seems to be a dialogue, although, as in " Fifine " and many others, one person
both quotes and answers the arguments of the second

The speaker asserts, "How very hard it is to be a Christian!" His friend apparently denies this, and the argument continues until the first relates a vision which appeared to him on Easter Eve three years before. He had been walking on the common past the little chapel, and as he walked he had been considering the question they had just argued. Finally, his reflections resolved themselves into the one question, "Am I any better because of the faith I profess? If the Judgment Day were to come now, should I be among those saved or lost?" As he had uttered these words aloud in the darkness, a sudden fire lit up the heaven, and a vision of the Christ appeared. The Judgment Day seemed to have come indeed, for the face was stern, and an austere voice declared the sentence passed, and heaven denied him. The voice spoke of how earthly joys had always filled his heart, and declared that so it should be still. The world with all it contained was left him, but heaven denied for ever. For a moment he rejoiced at the prospect of so much happiness as the world affords, but the voice sternly recounted all that he had lost, until with a desperate effort to resist despair, he declared that since faith in natural things was gone, the love and study of Art should replace it. At once the voice granted the desire, but again in words which made the gift seem valueless; and so he passed from one request to another, each granted as he spoke it, and each in turn made to seem valueless before God who stood in judgment. Then at the last, truth came to him, and he prayed for love of God and for faith, so that he might still hope on to reach "one eve the Better Land." Then the face relaxed its sternness, and he knew he was forgiven. Such was his evening vision, and he lives now happy in the

D

trials and temptations which he must bear and conquer,
rather than

> ".   .   .   .   .   left in God's contempt apart,
>   With ghastly smooth life, ...
>
>   .   .   .   .
>
>   .   .   .   .
>
>   .   .   .   .   .   .   shut
>   From heaven ! "

VI.—DRAMATIC LYRICS (1842).—*Cavalier Tunes*
comprise three stirring little lyrics, each vigorously
upholding King Charles I. and denouncing the Roundheads. They are named respectively: (1) *Marching
Along;* (2) *Give a Rouse;* (3) *Boot and Saddle.*

The Lost Leader is a dignified and tender lament over
the defection of a once honoured leader. Browning has
admitted that the poem bears actual reference to Words-
worth's abandonment of the Liberal cause.

How they brought the Good News from Ghent to Aix
is purely an imaginary story, but it is told so graphically
and realistically that no amount of truth could add to the
breathless interest which is excited by this fictitious
account of the three horsemen who start on their midnight ride to carry the *" Good News,"* and only one of
whom reaches Aix.

Through the Metidja to Abd-el-Kadr is chiefly interesting for the technical skill which Browning therein dis-
plays in expressing sense by sound. The repetition of
the same rhyme throughout the five verses, and the
metrical alternation of the short lines, convey not alone
the mere picture of the horseman riding through the
desert to rejoin Abd-el-Kadr, but an actual sense of the

swift, regular motion of the horse as it hastens towards the goal.

Nationality in Drinks is a bright little poem descanting on the relative merits of claret, tokay, and beer—the distinctive national drinks of France, Hungary, and England, and suggesting the fancies which each calls up.

GARDEN FANCIES.—I. *The Flower's Name* is the reverie of a lover on the garden across which his lady has walked with him a short time since, and especially on a certain flower, of which she had told the sweet lingering Spanish name.

II. *Sibrandus Schafnaburgensis* strikes a very different note. It is a comical account of a person who inflicts condign punishment on a book, because it is dry reading, by dropping it into the hollow of a tree, and there leaving it to the rain, toadstools, etc., which will make a home there. A month later he relents, and restores the poor, dilapidated volume to a place of comfort on his book-shelf. Mrs. Orr, in her Handbook, suggests that the title of the poem is probably the name of the author.

Soliloquy of the Spanish Cloister expresses with grim humour the hate which grows apparently through the absence of other passions. The speaker, a monk, launches every species of abuse and ridicule on a senior monk, Brother Laurence. His great hope is that some day the opportunity may arise to catch him tripping ; meanwhile, resenting both the content which Laurence derives from industrious gardening and the slight extra privilege which he enjoys in the convent, he consoles himself with destroying Brother Laurence's fruit trees and cultivating a sense of his own superior piety.

The Laboratory, on the contrary, describes a more acute

hate arising from the presence of other passions. A girl is buying poison, with which she means to destroy her rival, and from behind a glass mask she watches the preparation of the deadly powder with fiendish excitement and delight. Despised love and bitter hate rouse a storm of passions, which are the more vivid and intense by reason of the extreme concentration of the language. There is not a superfluous syllable, every word tells, and the whole scene is visible with awful clearness.

The Confessional pours forth with passionate eloquence the scorn and hatred for the Church, of a young girl who had been deceived by the priest into betraying political secrets of her lover, who thereby lost his life. Her frantic denunciations have now cost her her liberty, but she vows that, in spite of her prison cell, both God and man shall hear her accusing cry of grief and rage :

" Lies—lies, again—and still, they lie !"

Cristina is an expression of the ideal passion of love. The speaker has met Cristina, and at the first glance loved her with a perfect love, which shall illumine for him the dark journey of life. Cristina has expressed in one look the recognition of their mutual love but with her it was but a flash, which she has since lost, while with the man it remains a guiding star here, and, he firmly believes, hereafter. His is the ideal love which suffers all things, and is its own exceeding great reward.

The Lost Mistress is another example of the robust manner in which Browning treats his love-poems. The rejected lover bids farewell to his hopes of love and accepts friendship in its stead. There is a tone of sadness in his words, but neither reproach nor despair.

Earth's Immortalities consist of two little poems of only a few lines each, on the supposed immortality of Love and Fame. In each there is a touch of sarcasm and also of sadness.

Meeting at Night and *Parting at Morning* are companion pictures, of which love forms the motive. Two verses describe the glad anticipation of meeting, while four aptly significant lines express the necessary parting at morning when " the need of a world of men " returns.

Song is an exquisitely melodious little lyric in which a lover claims for his lady-love unqualified admiration and praise from even those who do not love her.

A Woman's Last Word is the voluntary sacrifice of her own individuality at the shrine of love. She has been quarrelling with her husband, who until now has been as a god to her, and she yields in the dispute, feeling that her individuality is of less value than the ideal she holds of her husband, which she must inevitably lose if they disagree. Thenceforth she promises she will mould her thoughts on his ; but, she adds, with gentle pathos, " That shall be to-morrow, not to-night," after she has been able to put sorrow away,

> " And so fall asleep, Love,
>   Loved by thee."

Evelyn Hope is one of the most beautiful poems in the English language. It is the lament of a middle-aged man over the dead body of a girl of sixteen whom he has loved. He was almost a stranger to her, and she neither knew of nor returned his affection. " It was not her time to love." But as he gazes on the " sweet, white brow," an inborn conviction springs up in his heart that it is not yet too late. God above " creates the love to reward the love," and hereafter, be it even after other lives have been lived, other worlds traversed, new knowledge gained and old knowledge lost, in the end she " will wake and remember and understand."

Love Among the Ruins is the reverie of a lover about to meet the girl he loves in a ruined tower close at hand, which is the sole remains of a once fabulously wealthy city. As the lover muses on this city, whence

> " In one year they sent a million fighters forth,"

he feels how little remains from all these centuries of " folly, noise and sin," and bids his heart

> " Shut them in,
> With their triumphs and their glories and the rest !
> Love is best."

A Lover's Quarrel is based on the belief that nothing in this world or the next can change true love. There is, therefore, even a vein of playfulness running through the lover's lament at the quarrel which has parted him from his love. He lives over again in fancy the happy days of three months before, when, despite the cold and dreary winter, sunshine born of love shone in their hearts. Now

> " The March sun feels like May !
>
> .　　.　　.　　.　　.　　.
> .　　.　　.　　.　　.　　.
>
> Only my love's away !
> I'd as lief that the blue were grey."

But as surely as the winter of the year will come round again in due course, so, he feels, will the summer sunshine of their love, and then all will be forgotten in the happy knowledge

"I shall have her for evermore !"

Up at a Villa—Down in the City is an extremely graphic description of the delights of a town life, as pictured by an Italian person of quality, who contrasts them piteously with the dead-and-alive kind of existence he leads at his country villa, but which he cannot afford to exchange for the town joys he longs for.

A Toccata of Galuppi's is at once the lightest and one of the most melodious and delicate of the Art-poems. The speaker is listening to a Toccata of Galuppi's, and the strains of the music conjure up before him the musician himself and the age (eighteenth century) in which he lived. The gay, careless life of the old Venetians rises before him, rebuked in vain by the solemn modulations of the music, and he grieves that the only outcome was mirth and folly, and no soul left " when the kissing had to stop."

Old Pictures in Florence is in praise of the old masters who had first abandoned the ideal models of Greek art, and began

> ". . . . to become now self-acquainters,
> And paint man man, whatever the issue !
> Make new hopes shine through the flesh they fray,
> New fears aggrandise the rags and tatters :
> To bring the invisible full into play !
> Let the visible go to the dogs—what matters ? "

The poem is framed in a humorous complaint that his admiration is never rewarded by finding those examples of them which exist unnoticed in Florence, and ends with a passionate prophecy of the extrusion of Austrian rule from Italy.

Home Thoughts from Abroad is an exquisite little song of exile, contrasting the delights of Nature in an English April and May with the gaudy flowers which the singer finds abroad.

Home Thoughts from the Sea expresses a burst of patriotic love for England, stimulated by the scenes of British victories, passed in coasting along the West of Spain. The four impressionist lines are exquisite.

Saul.—The first part is a semi-historical account of the Biblical narrative of how David, by his wondrous playing upon the harp and singing, won Saul from the melancholy to which he was subject. The poem is written as on the day following his visit to the king, when David reviews all that had occurred and puts it into speech, which on the previous day he had found impossible. He relates that for a long while he played and sang in vain. The king stood in the centre of the tent, motionless as death. Beginning with the simplest melodies, David played on and on, until at last the sound of the Levites' chant as they marched to the altar roused Saul with a groan from his lethargy. The groan shook the tent, but there was no other sign. Undaunted, David next sang of man's life, with its duties and pleasures, and gradually reached a climax in a direct appeal to Saul. Partial success rewarded the effort. The glare of madness faded from the king's eye, but the dull stare of despair remained. At this point (the end of the ninth stanza) the poem originally ended, the king's ultimate recovery being left to the reader's imagination. Ten years later, however, Browning completed the poem, making no mention of Saul, but adding to the Hebrew narrative the prophetic announcement of the birth of Christ.

By the Fireside.—Browning imagines himself in the

autumn of his life looking over his great Greek book and
turning to gaze at the image of his wife "reading by
firelight," that great brow

> " And the spirit-small hand propping it,
> Yonder, my heart knows how!"

Thence his thoughts will travel back to those parts of
Italy where he lived with her, recalling above all
the moment when in the solitude of the forests the
last faint screen between them was broken and intimate
friendship became love. In these memories he will
pass

> " An age so blest that, by its side,
> Youth seems the waste instead."

My Star tells of the insight given to loving eyes, and
denied to others. Browning did not think that Love is
blind.

Any Wife to Any Husband is the lament of a woman
who is dying, and who feels that, although her husband's
love has never failed during her life, it will nevertheless
not be strong enough to bear the test of separation. Her
grief at this thought is not of a selfish nature, for she is convinced that his actual love for her will not suffer; she regrets
the inevitable inconstancy which she foresees, merely as a
sign of weakness and lack of moral dignity in him.

Two in the Campagna is written in the form of a love-
poem, but it has regard not only to love, but to life itself.
It points out with mournful truth the insufficiency of
realisation as compared with the eternal longings of the
heart. Throughout the world, as with the lover in the
poem, we can obtain only " so much of our desires."

The lovers are together, their love is mutual, yet they are not content. There is an invisible barrier which prevents the absolute union of their souls, and it is the explanation of this unseen force which the man seems to discover. He illustrates his meaning by a spider's web, which he entreats his love, " Help me to hold," but which shrivels at his touch and vanishes. It appears to him that in this way he shall always just gain his goal, and as he seeks to grasp it, it will vanish ; and he discerns

> " Infinite passion, and the pain
> Of finite hearts that yearn."

Misconceptions is a cheery little poem, which describes how the fact that the beloved one meant no more by leaning for an instant on the man's heart than the bird meant by resting upon a certain spray before it flew to the top of the tree, does not alter the ecstasy of that instant.

A Serenade at the Villa begs the lady of the villa to understand her lover's absolute devotion, even though she cannot return his love, and not to prefer the silence of the hot thunderous night to the music of his voice and lute.

One Way of Love is a dainty little lyric, describing the way of perfect devotion with imperfect return.

Another Way of Love describes love wearied by too constant sweetness. The speaker here is the lady, and she tells her lover that, since he is weary of her incessant smiles, he is at liberty to go. She boasts, however, that if he tires of June roses, her June can more readily mend her bower than his hand can heal the scratches from the roses which he has gathered ; and then she will consider whether to bestow her roses on some one who appreciates their sweetness, or whether with another of June's attri-

butes—June lightning, to slay any spider whatever that
may approach her, and so, if we may break from the
metaphor, live an old maid all her life.

A Pretty Woman describes a woman who is nothing
but pretty, possessing no depth of feeling or power of
love. The speaker thinks that even such a woman serves
an end on earth. But to effect this end, men must take
her for what she is worth and leave her simply natural,
like the rose which loses its sweetness and true beauty
when copied in gold and jewels.

Respectability depicts the nightly walk of two lovers
on the banks of the Seine. They speak of the time
which would have been wasted before they found out the
true worth of the world and its good word, had, un-
happily, the world approved their union.

Love in a Life depicts a man who from youth to old
age searches for the twin soul whom he may love, and
finds life too short either to succeed in his quest or to
exhaust the possibilities of success. The world is typified
by a house, a simile which occurs more than once in
Browning.

Life in a Love presents the same man having found the
beloved one, but conscious that she will ever elude him,
and that the chase will take up his whole life.

In Three Days sounds the joyful note of expectant
love, over which thoughts of possible future dangers are
powerless to cast a gloom.

In a Year is a woman's heart-broken lament over her
lover's inconstancy.

Women and Roses is a dream in which the poet sees a
rose tree bearing three roses. A group of beautiful
women float round and round each. Around the first
rose, which is faded, move all the beautiful women of

ancient times; around the second, which is fresh and full, those of to-day; and around the third, a bud, those yet unborn. The poet appeals to each in turn to love him, but without answer they only float on, each round her own rose. The feeling with which the poem deals is that of the recognition of beauty which one can only watch from without, having no part in it. This feeling is most rare in Browning, and, perhaps, has been intentionally cast into a dream, in which sleep may be supposed to hold in bondage all powers but the power of watching.

Before and *After* are companion poems, of which the subject is a duel. A third person speaks "Before," urging that justice shall take its course, and shall thereby have avenged itself, whatever be the issue of the combat. If the wronged man be slain, he will have gained Heaven, and his murderer Hell, in the consciousness of sin which will pursue him throughout his life. If the guilty man fall, he will have atoned for his sin in death. Therefore, "Both the fighters to their places." They fight, and the sinner falls dead. "After," the victor gazes on the dead face once so dear to him, and he feels, too late, that death cannot erase the past, and in the present only adds remorse to his sorrow.

The Guardian Angel may best be described in Browning's own words as a "translation into song" of the picture, L'Angelo Custode, by Guercino, which hangs in the church of San Augostine at Fano. Together with a description of the picture is a record of the profound impression it made on Browning's mind.[1]

---

[1] The friend referred to in it is Alfred Domett, then in New Zealand. Cf. *Waring.*

Memorabilia is a tribute to the memory of Shelley, for whose poetry Browning had unbounded admiration.

Popularity is a perhaps finer, certainly more elaborate, poem in memory of Keats, whose fame and influence in the future are there foretold. To illustrate this future popularity and present obscurity, Browning imagines the fisherman who first landed the murex shell from which was obtained the deep blue dye that made the fortune of Tyre. Like Keats, the fisherman was obscure and un-rewarded ; but the source of beauty which he discovered brought undying glory to those who used it after him.

Master Hugues of Saxe-Gotha is the somewhat humorous soliloquy of an organist, supposed often to have played the fugues of the imaginary Master Hugues, and who now wishes to discover the absolute meaning which the com-poser read in the music. To this end he considers and describes with marvellous skill and aptness the construc-tion of a fugue, but still he can see nothing but a simple meaningless arrangement of five voices. This raises the suggestion that a fugue is symbolical of life in its complexity, beginning with one short phrase and leading through endless intricacies to where it began. But he feels that life has a higher meaning, although we cannot trace it in a fugue; and so farewell to fugues, and let a fuller, richer music, symbolical of the fulness and beauty of life, take its place. The descrip-tion in the course of the poem, of a fugue, is in every detail, as well as in general effect, absolutely accurate.

Luria, 1846, is a tragedy replete with noble thoughts nobly expressed, but it does not appeal so strongly to human interests and emotions as most of the other plays. Luria, a Moor in command of the army of Florence in a battle against Pisa, learns on the eve of the battle that while he is fighting in their cause, the Florentines at home have invented a charge of treachery against him, and in his absence are trying him for his life. This news is brought him by the Pisan general, who urges him to unite with Pisa in destroying Florence. Luria's simple, noble nature scarcely credits the alleged treachery, and in any case, refusing this revenge, he fights and wins the battle. Then he demands and learns the truth from Braccio, the Florentine Commissary, who has throughout the war been acting as a spy upon him. He is overwhelmed by despair at the unworthiness of the people he had so loved, takes poison, and dies at the moment when news is brought of his acquittal. The play is an excellent example of Browning's use of monologue, and, besides, contains some excellent character drawing. Braccio is a subtle sketch of the crafty Italian temper of the period. Feminine interest is introduced in Domizia, a Florentine lady, who seeks revenge on Florence for the unjust accusation of her two brothers. She rejoices that similar injustice is to be practised on Luria, because she hopes that he will avenge himself on her. His death, however, teaches her how little noble is revenge, and she determines to seek it no further.

VII.—*In a Balcony*, 1855, is a dramatic fragment left to the reader's imagination to place as a tragedy or drama.

Norbert, the Queen's chief minister, loves Constance, who is cousin to the Queen. Constance persuades him to tell the Queen of his love in such a way that she may think he only asks for Constance as the next best to herself, "since none loves queens directly, none dares that."

He reluctantly agrees, but overacts his part, so that the Queen takes his declaration to herself, and in wild excitement and delight seeks Constance, and tells her of her unhoped-for good fortune. Constance at once realises what has occurred, and, believing it to be for Norbert's advantage, determines to sacrifice herself, and yield him up to the Queen. The Queen leaves Constance, and Norbert comes, but before he understands, the Queen re-enters. Norbert proclaims his love for Constance in unmistakable terms, and the Queen, seeing how she has been deceived, leaves in silent rage. As the lovers embrace, the guards are heard approaching to arrest them. Browning has here reached a height of passion and tragic intensity such as he has only before attained in the great scene in " Pippa Passes." The words themselves are full of passion and power, but they are secondary to the supreme passion in the hearts of the two women. The contrast between the two is vivid. We are insensibly drawn to Constance because of her youth, her strong love, with its mistaken ideas of self-sacrifice, and perhaps because we feel that there are great possibilities in her soul, which are stunted in their development by the false and intriguing atmosphere of the Court. But a far more pathetic, heart-rending figure is the Queen in her solitary state dreaming for one bright moment that, old and unlovely, she is nevertheless blessed with love for which her soul has hitherto hungered in silence, and the next moment waking to find herself the victim, as she imagines, of an insulting plot.

DRAMATIS PERSONÆ (1864). — *James Lee's Wife* consists of a series of monologues spoken by the wife from the time when her mind grasps the first faint

glimmer of doubt as to her husband's love, until the con·
firmation of her fears when she leaves him. Passionate
love is evident in every word she utters, but it is also
clear how totally she and her husband misunderstand
each other. She is of a poetic and artistic temperament,
to which the need of love is paramount, and with this
she is ultra-sensitive and inclined to be morbid. The
husband (by inference, for we never hear him speak) is
essentially of this work-a-day world, and is absolutely
unable to grasp the ideal love and the poetic thoughts in
which his wife lives, and towards which she is for ever
trying to attract him. Her constant anxiety for his im-
provement wearies him, and he finds his pleasures away
from home. Thus they drift mentally further and further
apart, the wife's only idea of re-union being that her husband shall mould himself to her, and when at last we
find her " on deck," the thought uppermost in her mind
is that her silence will lead his heart back to her, and
that the parting is not for ever. The various phases of
mind through which James Lee's wife passes are depicted
in nine short poems.

I. *At the Window* she is watching for her husband's
return. The skies are changing towards winter, and
momentary dread fills her heart. Will her husband's
love change to winter also?

II. *By the Fireside.*—They are sitting together over
the fire, but she cannot silence her forebodings. She
thinks how the sailor out at sea will notice the brightly
lighted room and will envy the warmth within, and then
bitterly she contrasts the cheerful appearance of her home
with the dreary gloom in her own heart. The fire in
front of them is of shipwreck wood, and it seems to her
ominously suggestive of her life.

III. *In the Doorway.*—The cold of approaching winter, which makes the swallows flee and the leaves wither,
chills her heart. Then it braces her to a healthy resistance, and she resolves that her life and love shall not
change with the change of season.

IV. *On the Beach* is addressed directly to her husband,
but she seems to be speaking to his absent spirit rather
than to himself. She reviews the past, and reasons with
him, and endeavours to show him why he is in the
wrong. He first sought her love, and now that it is
wholly his, he not only despises but is angered by it.

V. *On the Cliff* she is struggling to hope against hope.
She watches a bare dry rock, which is suddenly beautified
by a butterfly which settles on it. In like manner, she
almost hopes love may beautify her husband's heart
and bring it back to her.

VI. *Reading a Book, Under the Cliff.*—The poem
which she here quotes is one which was published in a
magazine in 1836. It is a song indicating the wailing of
the wind, and attempting to fathom the meaning of the
sound, in which she finds the echo of her own grief. She
feels that her grief and the wind are alike controlled by
God, and she tries to submit patiently to His will, although she fails as yet to see the reason for the law of
change and uncertainty, the existence of which she cannot but admit.

VII. *Among the Rocks* she resigns herself to the inevitable, but determines that since

" If you loved only what were worth your love,
    Love were clear gain, and wholly well for you."

Therefore she will love on for ever, though her reward may
not be found on earth.

E

VIII. *Beside the Drawing-Board* completes the lesson of resignation which she began to learn among the rocks. She has for her models a little peasant-girl " with the poor coarse hand," and an exquisite cast of a hand by Da Vinci. For a moment she scorns the hand of flesh which is so unsightly, until she remembers that the beauty in Da Vinci's cast is due to his life-long study of all hands, coarse or otherwise. In like manner, she feels, must she study and endure life and reality ere she can produce the desired effect on her husband. And just as the poor coarse hand of the peasant is of equal use with the most beautiful, so must life without love be yet as useful and as earnest.

IX. *On Deck* is the fulfilment of this decision according to her lights. She feels that release from her presence is necessary to her husband's happiness, and therefore she is leaving him, but not without a faint hope that absence may endear her to him. Should this be, should he come to her at last with a gleam of love equal to her own, he might by then be old and wrinkled, ugly as herself, yet joy would blind her to everything but their re-union.

Gold Hair : A Story of Pornic, is a true story, and traces the effect of Original Sin in even those who appear most holy. A girl, supposed to be all that is good and gracious, was discovered, after her death, to have hoarded up and hidden in her golden hair, thirty gold pieces. To ensure that these should be buried with her, she assumed great pride in her masses of golden hair, and insisted that it should be left exactly as it was at her death.

The Worst of It is the passionate, heartbroken appeal of a man to his wife, who has been false to him. He implores her to return to the path of virtue, not to escape his anger, for, although he utterly resigns her here and hereafter, yet he feels for her nothing but an overwhelming sense of pity, which he knows will be powerless to avert God's wrath. The worst of it is that he is conscious of all the good which his wife's influence had formerly wrought upon him, and this recollection makes it the harder that he is helpless now, and can do nothing to save her.

Dis Aliter Visum ;[1] *or, Le Byron de Nos Jours,* is an indignant reproach spoken by a woman to the man who, ten years before, had seemed to love her, but who had lacked the moral courage to face the possible difficulties which might have arisen from the differences of their age and experience of life. He was already elderly, and she a girl. He had just allowed her to see the love which was dawning in his heart, then discretion had gained the day, and he had left her in silence. They have now met again for the first time, and with bitter irony, which we cannot but feel must have been born of love, she reviews the past ten years. He is still unmarried, is famous, and has become entangled with a ballet-dancer. She has married, but her life has been loveless, and thus the possibilities of her soul have been stunted, and her life infinitely narrowed. Thus the ruin of four souls lies at his door, and all the result of wasted opportunity.

Too Late is the lament of a lover who had not pressed his love, and had watched the beloved one give herself to another, while he still loved on in silence. Now it is too late. She is dead, and in death he feels that she is his own once more, as he believes she will be hereafter in eternity.

---

[1] "Heaven thought not so," from Virgil, Aen. II. 428.

Abt Vogler is a wonderful interpretation of the power of music. The Abbé has been extemporising upon the musical instrument which he had invented, and as the last notes die away, he is possessed of a passionate desire to retain the sounds of the music in his head, and in his soul the emotions and exaltation which it has called up. Out of it there had grown up a palace more beautiful than Solomon's, but it vanished like a dream. While it lasted the music bore him to the very heights of heaven and showed him all its glories, and the secrets of the past and future. But it is over now, and cannot be recalled. To him then music appears as "the finger of God," not "art in obedience to laws," and the cause of its power is unknown. Thus more nearly than all else in this world, music interprets the power of God. In God's eyes "There shall never be one lost good," but "All we have willed, or hoped, or dreamed of good shall exist," and therefore Abt Vogler is content to leave his music together with all other lost ideals, in God's hands, confident that our failure here is

"but a triumph's evidence
For the fulness of the days,"

and that hereafter we shall find them all perfected by God. With this comfort in his heart, Abt Vogler ceases to grieve at the suddenness with which the cessation of the music has brought him back to this lower world, the C major of life, and he finds rest.

Rabbi Ben Ezra expresses the supposed meditations on life and death of the Hebrew Rabbi of that name. According to him, life is to be a continual striving after the highest, which can only be reached in so-called death.

It is his belief that only in age does man begin to *know*, and that therefore it is contrary to all idea of God's love to think that just before success the end shall come to annul the labour of so many years. Thus he feels that death is but the perfecting crisis in the life of the soul which is immortal. Such is the bare outline of *Rabbi Ben Ezra*. It is one of those rare poems which go through the world helping to mould the lives of those who will fathom its meaning, a model of religious philosophy, giving strength and courage.

A Death in the Desert relates the death of St. John as supposed to be told by an eye-witness. The details of the surroundings of the dying apostle are graphically and delicately portrayed, and over the whole there hangs an atmosphere of calm in perfect harmony with a sacred death-bed.

St. John, the last of the disciples of Christ, has fled from persecution, and is hidden and guarded in a cave in the desert by faithful friends. His last hour is at hand, and he has lain long unconscious, but just before the end he recovers from his trance and speaks last words of counsel to those who are so tenderly watching him. He foretells the age of doubt which will ensue, when his very existence will not be credited and his life with Christ will be laughed to scorn; but he preaches courage to those who shall then be living, for he affirms that Christianity will never become a mere remembrance, because the indefinable need of love will never die ; and this need can be ascribed to no law of nature but only to God Himself. This idea seems to constitute the *raison d'être* of the poem. It is not historical, but seems to be a peg on which to hang the leading principles of Browning's religion. This is confirmed by the prophecy of modern

agnostic criticism, which Browning is well known to have
resented bitterly.

*Caliban upon Setebos: or Natural Theology in the
Island,* is a satire upon those who would create God in
their own image, and is an inimitable study of the
grotesque. Monologue is again the method of the poem,
which is written in the third person, after the manner in
which children speak. Caliban has stolen an hour's rest
from his labours, and while he sprawls in the sun to enjoy
it, he reflects somewhat disrespectfully on the God of
the Patagonians, Setebos, whom he worships. He explains his belief that Setebos is only a secondary deity,
and that there is One higher still whom Caliban styles
the "Quiet." Whether Setebos was created by the
"Quiet," Caliban cannot decide, but in any case he is
convinced that Setebos is not the primary deity, and
therefore Caliban imputes to him human attributes and
weaknesses, and imagines him jealous of the "Quiet,"
just as he, Caliban, is jealous of Setebos. Suddenly a
thunderstorm begins, and in terror Caliban hides his
face, protesting infinite penitence for disrespect, and
promising anything and everything if only he may escape
the dreadful thunder.

Confessions.—The speaker is dying, and his answer to
the priest's inquiry as to whether he does not "view the
world as a vale of tears" is a review of the love episode
of his youth, in which with exultant joy he lives over
again the happiness of long ago. In the description of
the scene of the love-making, in order to fix the spots
which he used to pass, the sick man points to the position of various medicine bottles on the table, and it is
remarkable that there is nothing grotesque in this
commonplace illustration. Rambling on with the

story, the two last lines sufficiently express the spirit
of the poem,

> " How sad and bad and mad it was—
> But then, how it was sweet ! "

May and Death is a lament on the death of a friend.
The mourner wishes that the season which has robbed
him of his friend might in turn be robbed of all its
beauty. Then, realising the selfishness of such a wish,
he modifies it, and only wishes that one plant might die
which specially reminds him of his dead friend.

Deaf and Dumb, a Group by Woolner.—The faces
and eyes of the deaf and dumb children in Woolner's
group express what their lips could not adequately have
spoken, just as the obstruction of the prism divides blank
white light into its lovely elementary colours.

Prospice is a passionate protest against fear of death.
It is a tribute to the memory of Mrs. Browning, written
only a few months after her death, and the knowledge
that it is a personal utterance adds to its interest, although
not to its beauty, which nothing can enhance.

Eurydice to Orpheus interprets Sir Frederick Leighton's
picture of that name, and puts into the mouth of Eurydice
such pleading words that she appears entirely responsible
for Orpheus' disobedience in turning to look at her.

Youth and Art has for motive, like " Dîs Aliter
Visum," the pathetic utterance, " What might have
been," but this poem is written in a much lighter and
almost humorous spirit. The woman is again the
speaker, but there is no bitterness in the speech, only a
vague regret.

A Face describes with infinite delicacy and grace the
picture of a very beautiful head and throat.

A Likeness expresses the annoyance which is caused by the indifferent criticism of some object precious to its owner. The instance quoted is that of a print which has been bought for the sake of some fancied resemblance, and which a friend, ignorant of the association, half-heartedly admires or takes exception to.

Mr. Sludge, the Medium, is a sketch supposed to be founded on an incident in the life of the American spiritualist, Home. The poem is extremely humorous, and, at the same time, is a striking instance of Browning's sympathy with all men—that is to say, of his power of realising what in given circumstances their thoughts would be, whether he shares them or no. It is quite certain that Browning in no way felt with such an acknowledged cheat and humbug as Sludge, but he insists that even he shall have fair play, and allows him at least to defend himself. Discovered cheating in the house of his patron, Mr. Hiram Horsfall, Sludge ingeniously turns the tables on to Society, affirming that truth is not believed, and that therefore lies are actually forced from him. By arguments expressed with infinite humour, Sludge confesses, excuses, and defends himself to such effect that his patron pardons him, and even dismisses him with a present of money. Left alone, Sludge changes his tone, and departs cursing Mr. Horsfall freely, and vowing vengeance.

Apparent Failure, a touching little poem on the Morgue[1] at Paris, is one of the many examples of Browning's optimism and of his firm faith in the immortality of the soul. He had visited the Morgue, and the sight of the bodies of three suicides, which many would have

---

[1] The building where the bodies of those found drowned are carried for identification.

shrunk from in disgust, only calls from him exclamations of pity, and the expression of his belief

" That what began best, can't end worst,
    Nor what God blessed once, prove accurst."

Epilogue presents a kind of summing up of religion in all its aspects. The first speaker, as David, represents the strong faith of Judaism, and testifies how, amidst the worship of thousands, the presence of the Lord filled the house of the Lord. Next comes Renan, grieving over the loss of Christian faith, which he thinks has gone to join other myths, and over the hard responsibility of those who have to lead men's thoughts in default of religion. Lastly comes Browning himself, who declares God's earth to be the only temple needed for His worship, and that God is my universe that feels and knows.

VIII., IX., X.—*The Ring and the Book.*—"The Ring and the Book" may best be described as a gigantic dramatic monologue in twelve books. It has its origin in an old Roman murder case, the account of which Browning found in a book he bought for eightpence at a second-hand bookstall in Florence. In it he found not only the details of the murder, but also verbatim copies of the speeches for and against the accused, together with the final judgment of the Pope, and certain manuscript letters reporting the execution of the murderers. It has often been urged that the story is not a fit subject for poetry, and at first sight of the bare details this seems true. Browning himself realised this, and he defends his choice in the first part of the poem, to which he gives the title of the whole—" The Ring and the Book."

The following epitome of the story may serve as a guide to the plot and the construction.

Count Guido Franceschini, an impecunious nobleman of Rome, is anxious to retrieve his shattered fortunes by a wealthy marriage, and to this end he takes for his wife Pompilia, the supposed child of Pietro and Violante Camparini. This couple, thinking to secure for themselves a luxurious shelter for their old age, do not undeceive Guido as to Pompilia's parentage until the marriage has taken place, and the expected dowry is claimed. Then each party discovers his mistake. The Comparini promptly find that discretion is the better part of valour, and quit their adopted son-in-law's not too hospitable roof, leaving poor Pompilia to bear the brunt of his rage. This is no light matter, and she seeks alleviation of her miseries in vain. The Church and the law, to whom she appeals, alike rebuke and send her back to her husband, and she submits patiently to his malice until she realises that ere long she will become a mother. Then, with the courage of despair, she leaves her husband's house, escorted by her own true friend, Giuseppe Caponsacchi, a priest of Arezzo. Guido pursues and overtakes them at Castelmurio, and they are arrested. The case is tried, but Guido's charge against his wife of infidelity not being proved, Caponsacchi is merely banished for a time, while Pompilia is consigned to the care of a sisterhood, and is eventually permitted to return to Violante and Pietro.

Here a son is born, who is at once hidden away in safety out of his father's reach. A fortnight later, Guido, accompanied by four hired assassins, makes his appearance at the Comparini's villa, attacks and kills them both, together with Pompilia, who, however, survives long enough to give evidence of the crime. Guido is arrested the same night, and boldly admits his deed, defending it on the alleged ground of his wife's infidelity, which, he declares, renders the murder a simple act of justice. Pompilia's innocence, however, is fully proved, and Guido is condemned. He makes a final appeal to the Pope, who utterly refuses him mercy, and the sentence of death is carried out.

Such is the bare outline of the story, in the minute investigation of which Browning has filled four volumes and 20,000 lines. One might reasonably expect from this statement that the constant repetition of the tale would become wearisome; and that it never does become so is sufficient evidence of the subtle genius which produced the work. For character painting and grouping it is unrivalled in English literature, and it is difficult to fitly criticise such passages as that at the close of the first book, beginning

"O, lyric love, half-angel and half-bird,"

wherein the poet invokes in his work the help and blessing of his dearly-loved wife, who had died some years before, but whose soul he feels death has left unchanged, and whose spirit is ever with him. The action of the entire poem takes place during the period of the trial of Guido's subsequent appeal to the Pope.

The Ring and the Book opens with a description of the manufacture of a gold ring, and the reader is at once told that this dissertation on the manner of moulding the gold into a circlet is analogous to Browning's plan of

moulding the facts of the murder case into a poem. Gold
alone is too soft for such delicate workmanship, and is,
therefore, mixed with alloy to make it durable. So with
the poem. The book he bought for eightpence is the
pure golden fact too soft for use as it is, but easy to work
into the desired form when alloyed with a new spirit—
that of the poet's self. To this end, writes Browning,

"I fused my live soul and that inert stuff,"

until one by one the scenes rose before his eyes no
longer dead words, but tragedies of living, breathing
men and women. Next follows a plain unvarnished
account of the case just as set forth in the book, and after
this come the various points of view from which Browning intends to consider the trial. Public opinion is
accorded the first claim, and is, of course, divided in its
mind. Hence we find the verdicts of *Half Rome*,
which favours the husband's cause; *The Other Half
Rome*, which indignantly defends the wife; and *Tertium
Quid*, in which the speaker is addressing two persons of
high degree, of whose opinions he is not quite sure.
Tertium Quid is, therefore, careful not to commit himself
on either side, but merely proposes the arguments each
might use. Rome and rumour having thus spoken, next
come the *dramatis personæ* of the tragedy. First, *Count
Guido Franceschini*, just released from the rack, speaking
with assumed humility, tells his tale. He admits and
glories in his deed, which he asserts was an act of justice
due to the Church, of which he declares himself a most
zealous adherent. Weaving together a tissue of false-
hoods, he only introduces truth where it can be turned to

his advantage. With exquisite craft he turns and twists his defence to appeal to the susceptibilities of his judges, elaborating such arguments as he thinks likely to gain their sympathy, and slurring over those which his assumed innocence forces him to name, but which he knows would weaken his case. This marriage, according to his version, was a matter of arrangement, in which love had no part, and he at least had faithfully adhered to the terms of the agreement, although he had been so shamefully duped in the matters of Pompilia's birth and dowry. He implies that, nevertheless, had she cared to try, Pompilia might have aroused some feeling of affection in him, but she did not try, and of that he will not complain. The true motives for his killing her was his devotion to the Church, whom her infidelity had insulted, and his own outraged feelings as a father, on which last point he dwells largely. Finally, he defies the Court to convict him justly, and after an eloquent appeal that his son, together with his wounded honour, should be restored to him, he makes way for his alleged rival. *Giuseppe Caponsacchi's* evidence forms a finely-drawn contrast to Count Guido's. It lacks the overwhelming spirit of intellectual genius which pervades the Count's oration, but instead it has a ring of truth which invests its pathos and passion with power not less impressive. Caponsacchi speaks in a state of violent agitation, which he tries vainly to suppress. He can hardly credit the news of the murder, which, with a summons to appear at the trial, has brought him from Civita Vecchia, and when he at last grasps the truth, his soul is torn with conflicting emotions of rage and sorrow. Distress and indignation fill his heart, and with passionate fervour he relates the story of his whole acquaintance with Pompilia from his first sight of her at the theatre until their flight. Then, fearing lest his reverence and devotion for her may through his vehemence be miscon-strued into unholy love, he tries to moderate his words and speak with forced calm. At the last with a cry of utter despair he leaves the Court.

Pompilia.—-The next scene takes place by the bedside of the dying Pompilia, who, in touching, child-like words tells the story of her life—such a simple, gentle little life, without the experience that might have brought her worldly wisdom. Married at thirteen to a man nearly four times her own age, she had expected her husband to love and cherish her "as husbands are supposed to," and disappointed in this, she none the less knew her duty to obey her husband; and so in patience and submission she obeyed until she knew another life than hers was in her hands. Then, at the mother's call, the woman in her sprang to life. For her unborn child no sacrifice or risk could be too great, and she sent for Caponsacchi. The forged letters which the waiting-woman had carried between them were nothing to her, for she could neither read nor write. Her husband's furious tirades against Caponsacchi did not trouble her. In her new joy, the solitary joy which had shone upon her life, her instinct fastened upon her one true friend, and without doubt or fear she turned to him for help. After that, until her husband's savage slaughter at the villa, every-thing had seemed a dream in which the one reality had been her child, and even this is taken from her. Still with exquisite pathos she thanks God that he was born, and that for a whole long fortnight he was hers. Of her husband she speaks as little ill as she can, and merely says, "I could not love him, but his mother did." So to the end, when her last words are *m* blessing of her "soldier-saint" who "saved her at her need."

From the supreme beauty of Pompilia we turn with reluctance to the most matter-of-fact portions of the poem, the counsel for the prosecution and the counsel for the defence. The change of atmosphere is somewhat abruptly evident in the very first lines of *Dominus Hycinthus de Archangelis,* of which the metre and versification at once denote an almost humorous spirit. De Archangelis is preparing his speech in defence of Count Guido's crime, but beneath his Law and Latin there runs an under-current of domestic matters which is highly amusing, although somewhat irritating immediately after the hushed and tender pathos of Pompilia's tale. To the advocate, however, the feast in honour of his son's eighth birthday is more interesting than Count Guido, and his chief object is to get through his work quickly, so that he may the sooner enjoy a romp with his little son. His arguments are therefore merely words strung together, with which for a show of learning he mixes a great deal of Latin. He assumes Pompilia to be guilty, so takes no pains to prove it, and then by much obviously false reasoning he asserts the justice of Count Guido's avenging his outraged honour. *Juris Doctor Johannes Baptista Bottinius,* the Fisc or public prosecutor, is equally unenthusiastic over his case, and is merely anxious to defeat De Archangelis, of whom he is extremely jealous. His ideal of womanhood is evidently low, and his defence of Pompilia consists more in coarse praise of her and in attempting to justify the misconduct which is alleged against her than in denying it. It seems probable that Bottinius was not fully convinced and was wholly indifferent as to her innocence.

His object is simply to advertise himself, which he does
in an amusing if rather repulsive manner.

The Pope.—From these—the least interesting sections
of the poem—we pass to one of the most impressive, the
summing-up and final verdict of the Pope. The grave,
measured verse in which this book is written admirably
portrays the dignity and solemnity which may well be
supposed to characterise Pope Innocent XII. We find
him at the end of a long day which has been devoted to
earnest consideration of Count Guido's case. He has
arrived at his final decision, that the murderers shall be
put to death; but before he puts the seal to this decree,
he pauses and reviews the case yet once again, fearing
lest his mere human judgment may err. To avert such
mishap he searches for precedent in the past, but finds
each a contradiction of the last. On himself alone then
he must rely; and he is an old man whose end cannot be
far distant, and from whose weary shoulders he would
fain keep the burden of this fellow-mortal's death. On
what plea dare he grant mercy? He lays bare the inmost workings of his heart and mind, from which his
judgment has been formed, and the result is that he feels
his decision to be the right one, "in the eyes alike of
God and man." As he reviews the case, he throws a
new light upon it by reiterating the points upon which
Guido based this last appeal, but he turns these very
arguments of defence into weapons against the Count.
Guido had pleaded for a reprieve on the ground of his
connection with the Church, and of his high birth.
But these advantages, argues the Pope, only increase
his guilt, while the dishonour of Pompilia's birth
sheds added radiance on her purity and goodness, since
from the child of such a mother surely evil only might

have been expected.   With tender, reverential words
the old man rejoices in the "one blossom makes me
proud at eve," ending

> "Go past me
> And get thy praise,—and be not far to seek
> Presently when I follow if I may!"

Caponsacchi he places "not so very much apart," but
awards him a more qualified praise, feeling that, although
he has done well and wisely in coming to Pompilia's
rescue, yet he has not done so in a manner entirely con-
sistent with the dignity of the Church.   For Guido he
can see no hope here or hereafter, unless the suddenness
of the shock of death may flash the truth into his soul
and save him.   He bids Pietro and Violante "troop
somewhere 'twixt the best and worst," for he realises that
they sinned more through ignorance than vice, and they
have suffered for their sin.   Thus having judged the actors
in the drama, and having sought in prayer true light from
God, Pope Innocent silences his inclination to pity with
one question, "How should I dare die, this man let live?"
The next line shows the answer which his conscience
makes:—

> "Carry this forthwith to the Governor!"

Guido.—The next book, the last of the monologues
spoken by the characters of the drama, brings us back
again to Guido; but, as Browning makes evident by his
title, it is the man himself this time who speaks, not
the smooth-tongued hypocrite, Count Guido Franceschini.
Guido has received the final judgment of the Pope,
but can scarcely credit its reality.   As the truth forces
itself upon him, he tries, with protestations of innocence,
to persuade his former friends, Cardinal Acciaiuoli and

F

Abate Panciatichi, to intercede once again for his life, but all to no purpose. The time for any chance of reprieve is past, the hour of doom is rapidly drawing near, and they are there to receive Guido's confession and to shrive him. Guido's last hope dies away, and as it dies he throws off the mask with which he had hoped to cheat his judges. The Cardinal and Abate desire his confession? They shall have it, and truth itself does indeed appear. But such truth, such confession ! Frantic with rage and despair, the unhappy man pours forth a torrent of blasphemy, impenitence, and scorn, very different from his specious, wary speech before the Court. Raving in alternate bursts of defiance and entreaty, his last moments pass, until, as the door opens and the guard enters to lead him to execution, an involuntary confession of his wife's innocence is wrung from his dying lips in his last frenzied cry,

" Abate,—Cardinal,—Christ,—Maria,—God, . . .
    Pompilia, will you let them murder me ? "

The Book and the Ring.—Under this title follows what may be described as author's notes on the preceding eleven books, together with four letters, part genuine, part fictitious, describing the execution of Count Guido and his accomplices. The first letter, from a Venetian gentleman to a friend, describes the execution among the news of the past week. The second, from De Archangelis, the late Count's counsel, is diplomatically written for the edification of the late Count's friends and relations, and dwells upon the noble bearing and patience of the Count until the end, together with much more in a similar strain. To this, however, Browning adds an imaginary postscript, which is evidently intended for only one pair of eyes, and this is to quite another effect. In it the writer admits that his only regret for the Count's death is that it involves his own failure and consequent lack of pay. At the same time he confides to his friend that the Gomez case, which is soon coming on, will make up for this one proving unprofitable. The third letter is again imaginary, and comes from Bottinius, Pompilia's counsel. His chief regret is that his case was so easily won. He would have relished a harder fight better. As to Pompilia's innocence or guilt, that interested him but little, and now fancying that he sees an advantage to be gained by her guilt, he proceeds to declare that Guido's guilt in no way proves her innocence, which he attempts to disprove. By this he hopes to secure her property for the monastery to which she was originally consigned, and from which he hopes to receive a large reward. It is interesting to know that, although the letter to this effect is fictitious, such an attempt was actually made. The Pope interfered to prevent this, and Browning quotes from the actual verdict on the matter, as recorded in the little yellow-covered eightpenny book in which he discovered all the other details of the case.

Last, but not least, come Browning's own reflections on the story and on the probable fate of Pompilia's child, together with the statement that the object of the whole poem is to prove the worthlessness of human testimony. Finally, the poet lays his rounded ring at the feet of the "Lyric Love," whose help and blessing he had invoked at the close of the first book.

XI.—*Balaustion's Adventure, including a transcript from Euripides.*—*Balaustion's Adventure* is written with a double motive; in the first place as a vindication of the power of poetry, and secondly to introduce the transcript of the *Alkestis* of Euripides. Its first object is attained melodiously, and with an enthusiasm which irresistibly communicates itself to the reader.

Balaustion tells her girl-friends the story of how she and her companions from Rhodes were pursued by a pirate ship and sought for shelter in the harbour of Syracuse. This was refused, until Balaustion, knowing their love for Euripides, volunteered to recite to them his play of *Alkestis*, as she had recently seen it performed at Kameiros. Having recounted her adventure, through which, she says, she has gained not only her freedom but the esteem of Euripides himself and the love of Euthykles, Balaustion proceeds to recite the play to her friends.

Alkestis.—Admetus, the husband of Alkestis, was dying, but according to a promise which Apollo had gained for him from the Fates, his life might be spared if some friend would voluntarily die in his stead. His wife accordingly sacrificed herself, and then, too late, he repented of his selfish cowardice. His whole household was plunged in grief when Herakles,[1] not knowing of Alkestis' death, came jubilantly to visit him. Admetus told him that death was in the house, but did not say who was dead. Nevertheless Herakles at once proposed to proceed to some other host. This Admetus would not allow, and bade his servants prepare the guest-rooms and "furnish forth a plenteous feast." While feasting, Herakles learnt from a servant that it was Alkestis who was dead. Touched by Admetus' courtesy and hospitality in the midst of his own grief, Herakles resolved to descend into Hades and wrestle with Death for Alkestis. He re-

---

[1] Hercules.

turned panting but victorious, bearing Alkestis, veiled, with him. He then asked Admetus' protection for the woman he had brought, and it was not until he was convinced of the sincerity of his penitence for his late cowardice that he showed him that the woman was his own wife.

The translation of the *Alkestis* is declared by Greek scholars to be admirable, although it is here reproduced as an epic poem, not a play. Browning's own criticisms and explanations by the way bring out the sympathetic humanity of Euripides.

Balaustion herself leaves a happy, refreshing memory in our minds, and we look forward with pleasure to her re-appearance in *Aristophanes' Apology*.

Prince Hohenstiel-Schwangau, Saviour of Society.— *Prince Hohenstiel-Schwangau* is a fictitious monologue supposed to be spoken by Louis Napoleon, and is a clever mixture of justice and sophistry. The scene of the poem is laid in a room near Leicester Square, where the Prince sits smoking and drinking tea with an adventuress, to whom he volunteers to relate the history of his political life and to explain the motives which have induced his line of conduct. He begins by stating that he assumes the title *Saviour of Society* in contra-distinction to the would-be *reformers* of Society ; because, while the latter have endeavoured to bring about a new state of things, he has merely laboured to preserve and make the best of the old. He cites and defends not only possible accusations launched against him by the world, but also the arguments of his own conscience.[1] His defence of his mode of life is brilliant special-pleading, and is most in-

---

[1] Cf. the husband in *Fifine* and Aristophanes in *Aristophanes' Apology*.

teresting : nevertheless it always leaves a feeling that it is only talk, and although much of what he asserts is both true and laudable in theory, the poem seems to reach a perfectly natural ending in the admission that neither his life nor his defence of it are entirely satisfactory even to himself.

Fifine at the Fair discusses the merits of a vagrant and unconventional life with particular regard to inconstancy in marriage. The advantages and justifications are set forth in an elaborate monologue in the body of the poem, addressed by the speaker to his wife ; and the final judgment of the poet seems to be set out in the *Epilogue*, spoken by the same speaker, in which he imagines how, years after his wife's death, he, being himself about to die, sees only his wife returning to re-union with him. In the *Prologue* the poet imagines a swimmer in the sea, while a butterfly floats through the air over his head ; and he feels that as each of them is in a separate element, and yet is conscious of and can watch the other, so it may be that those in heaven watch mortals left behind on earth. In the poem itself the husband continues this simile of a swimmer in the sea. He speaks of his wife, Elvire, as the sea itself, while Fifine, the gipsy, represents simply the froth of the waves, valueless in itself, yet without which the sea would be incomplete. Having thus vindicated the necessity for Fifine's existence, he proceeds to show the special use she is to be to him. She, Fifine the foam-flake, here one minute, gone the next, if gathered useless and not even beautiful, is to give him an impetus towards Elvire, the very ocean which never varies or slips away. When every argument fails to convince Elvire, he makes a last effort to gain his point by describing to her a dream he has had of the Carnival at Venice. At first he seemed to view it from a distance, and could not understand what the revellers were saying, and everything looked grotesque and ugly. As he drew nearer, the faces and language became clearer and more human, and at last by mixing with the crowd he understood the worth of qualities which at first sight he had counted as faults. Then in his dream he grew aware that the supposed Carnival was in reality the world, and that the nearer he drew to the men and women in it, the less repulsive did they become. At this he awoke filled with the determination that henceforth "nothing human should be alien to him," and he declares that it is in the exercise of this lesson that he now urges the claims of Fifine. While he is speaking, as if to show the value of his reasoning, a note is slipped into his hand. He explains to Elvire that he had given Fifine gold in mistake for silver, and he begs five minutes in which to "clear the matter up." If he exceeds that time, he declares that Elvire may indeed doubt and leave him. With this the body of the poem ends abruptly, and the *Epilogue*, in a solemn, musical measure, sums up its discussion with "love is all and death is naught."

XII.—*Red Cotton Nightcap Country ;* or, *Turf and Towers*, 1873.—This poem derives its title second-hand from Miss Thackeray, who had laughingly styled St. Aubin, the actual scene of this drama of real life, White Cotton Nightcap Country, on account of its dead-and-alive appearance, and also from the custom among its inhabitants, both men and women, of wearing white caps. In 1872, Browning and Miss Thackeray met at St. Aubin (called in the poem St. Rambert), and here Browning took occasion to correct the title, White Cot·

ton Nightcap Country, to Red Cotton Nightcap Country,
as being more suitable to the tragic tale he knew concerning it.   The conversational method of the poem
gives a lighter tone and an added interest to a
somewhat gloomy tale, of which, unfortunately, the details are absolutely true, the only fictitious items being
imaginary names instead of real ones.   The story is that
of Léonce Miranda,[1] who committed suicide on his
estate at St. Aubin in 1870.   A man of Spanish descent
and temperament, Miranda was governed by two conflicting passions : the strongest devotion to the Catholic
Church, and utter infatuation in the love of a lady, Clara
Mulhausen.   An inconvenient husband was the obstacle
which prevented Miranda from reconciling his two passions.   He therefore chose the lady, and lived with her
in what would have been perfect happiness but for the
opposing passion, which disturbed his conscience.   After
five years of this kind of life, during which he spent
much time and money on improving his estate, his
mother suddenly sent for him to remonstrate severely on
his extravagance.   Miranda was much attached to his
mother, and felt her reproof so keenly that he attempted
suicide by throwing himself into the Seine.   He was
rescued ; but, despite every care, he lay at death's door
until Clara was summoned to his side, after which he
gradually recovered sufficiently to return with her to St.
Aubin.   Before he was perfectly convalescent, however,
he was again summoned to his mother's house.   There
he found her dead, and a tribe of cousins waiting to
pounce upon her property, and to din into his ears their
opinion that he alone was responsible for her death.

---

[1] Antoine Mellerio, the jeweller of the Place Vendôme, Paris.

Their cruel words had the desired effect. Miranda fell into a swoon, and, on recovery, agreed to sign a deed of gift, distributing all his property among his relations, reserving only a sufficient portion for Clara, from whom he determined to part forever. On the very day, however, on which the deeds were to be finally signed and sealed by himself and Clara, Miranda was found delirious before a huge fire, in which it was his evident intention to destroy himself, and from which he was dragged away, raving that he was being deprived of his last chance of salvation. His hands had already been burnt away, and his condition was such that when the delirium left him several months of complete prostration ensued. Immediately on his recovery he returned to Clara, and his cousins heard no more about the distribution of his property among themselves. For two years he endeavoured by the strictest regard for all religious observances and by fabulous acts of indiscriminate charity to atone for the illegal love to which he still clung. Then suddenly, without apparent rhyme or reason, he one day flung himself from the top of the tower in his garden, and was found dead below.

Browning, after the large-hearted manner in which he sympathised with all mankind, attributes the fatal leap not to suicidal intent, but to a fanatical desire to vindicate the power of the Image which is worshipped as a god in France, on account of its supposed power of working miracles. He conceives Miranda's hope to have been that by supernatural power he would leap from the tower to the church opposite, in which the Image stood, and that by so doing he would prove indisputably to sceptics the infallibility and glory of the Church. The poem is written in flowing blank verse, which seldom rises to passion.

but which is always just full enough of energy and spirit to keep the reader's interest thoroughly alive. The characters of Miranda and Clara being taken from life, there is little scope for imagination in their portrayal, but it is remarkable with what unerring aim Browning has probed their hearts and read the story of their inner lives. Miranda presents by far the more finished sketch, Clara being to a great extent merely his reflection. Both her final speech to the cousins who intrude upon her after Miranda's death, and his soliloquy just before he takes the fatal leap, are imaginary, and are fine examples of dignity and repressed power.

The Inn Album, 1875, is a notable example of Browning's attraction towards grotesque subjects, in which he found such deep psychological interest. It also bears out admirably his favourite saying, "nihil humanum alienum a me puto," since the bare details of the story (unfortunately a true one) are repulsive in the extreme. Yet so skilfully has he wrought the touch of Nature into what would else be mere vulgar crime, that disgust is replaced by interest, and immorality loses half its horror in tragic grandeur. The story could not well have been reproduced with the exactitude which characterises *Red Cotton Nightcap Country*, and for this reason as well as for poetical purposes Browning has closed the poem with the violent death of the nobleman whose wickedness forms the basis of the story. In reality the man lived for many years after the events treated of in the poem. Browning also introduces the imaginary character of a young girl who, though a mere sketch in herself, forms the pivot on which the tragedy of the other three characters turns. These other three characters are taken from life, but all four are nameless in the poem and are dis-

tinguished only as the "elder" or "younger" man and
woman. The younger man has been transformed from
the low gambler which he really was into a youthful hero
caught in the toils of an experienced villain, and as such
he becomes a subject of interest and sympathy. There
is great pathos in the simple-minded, honest young fellow
who discovers in the victim of his friend's treachery his
own lost love, for whom his old reverence and devotion
are as strong as ever, though they are mixed with pity
now. The elderly *roué*, with his long record of sin and
shame, in which he sees only lost opportunities that rouse
regret but no remorse, is a perfect study of innate wickedness. Even his own passionate appeal that his former
victim shall forget her past and present life and fly with
him to a happy future is only a fresh insult, although it
is possible that the sudden and unexpected meeting may
have roused in him a momentary flash which he believed
to be genuine love. The sequel, however, proves the
utter baseness of the man who endeavours to sell her to
his friend as payment of a gambling debt, and who
threaten , should she refuse, to lay before her unsuspecting
husband the history of her past life.

The lady herself presents a far simpler picture. Her
experi nce of wasted love and trust has crushed her life
and c inged her nature. Love had ruled her very soul,
and i betrayal turned it into hate. It is not that she
seeks to claim undeserved sympathy : she realises that
her own sin has brought a ji : inishment, from which
there 's no escape except in dea .. It seems as if, in spite
of th past, she had not fully grasped the infamy of her
sometime lover until he makes his foul suggestion. Then
all th t is best in her nature rises in a desperate effort to
save the youth who has so chivalrously loved her from

the clutches of his false, evil-minded friend. With heart-felt earnestness she implores him to resist the fatal influence which has been her ruin, and will be his, if he has not strength enough to throw it off now and forever. Profoundly moved, although at first bewildered, the youth yields to her appeal, and when the truth is clear to him, his vengeance is swift and sure.

XIII.—*Aristophanes' Apology*, 1875, shows us Balaustion happily married, having seen her hero-poet, and received from him the priceless gift of his tragedy, *Herakles.* Euripides is now dead, and as they float towards Rhodes, Balaustion recalls to her husband, Euthykles, the events of the night on which they first heard of their poet's death. Balaustion had been about to commemorate the night by reading aloud his *Herakles,* when a knock at the door, followed by shouts of merriment, bade them open to Aristophanes. He entered drunk, and with mock deference explained the object of his visit. His play, *Thesmophoriazusæ,* had been a great success, and while the uproarious mirth of the supper which followed it was at its height, Sophocles had entered, and announced the death of Euripides. Aristophanes, feeling half guilty because of his previous ridicule and abuse of the dead poet, had felt the need of justifying himself, and therefore had come to Balaustion and Euthykles, whom he regarded as almost belonging to Euripides. His apology, Balaustion continues, was a defence of comedy as the best means of teaching truth, while doing harm to none, and he had explained his objections to Euripides, and challenged her to defend him. This she did, first in her own words, and then by what she thought the most powerful of all means, the reading of the *Herakles*, which Aristophanes' arrival had interrupted. By this time their boat is nearing Rhodes, and the poem ends with a final tribute to Euripides, in Balaustion's emphatic assertion that he will live forever, and her thanksgiving, " Glory to God, who saves Euripides ! "

Euripides' tragedy of *Herakles (Hercules Furens)* opens with the return of Herakles from Hades, whence he has brought Cerberus.[1] He finds his wife and children in sore distress, thinking him dead, and themselves threatened with death by the usurper Lukos. Herakles slays Lukos, but is afterwards seized with a fit of madness, in which he kills his wife and children. When he recovers his senses he is overwhelmed with grief at what he has done, and the play ends with his departure with Theseus, King of Athens, who vainly endeavours to rouse and comfort him.

Aristophanes' Apology is more difficult to understand than *Balaustion's Adventure*, on account of the many classical allusions ; but the main thread of the story can be followed and enjoyed by the most unclassical reader.

The Agamemnon of Æschylus, 1877, is the hardest of all Browning's Greek poems. The plot is familiar to most. Agamemnon returns from Ilion to Argos with Cassandra, the prophetess. His wife, Clytemnestra, jealous of his love for Cassandra, and enraged at the sacrifice of his daughter, Iphigenia, slays Cassandra, while her lover, Aigisthos, kills Agamemnon. Browning has made a perfectly literal translation of the play, which is, however, more remarkable for its exactness of word for word in almost the original metre than for its poetic beauty.

XIV.—*Pacchiarotto and other poems.—Prologue* is a

---

1 This was the last of his twelve labours.

dedication to a lady, in which Browning speaks of himself as breaking forth with his tale through the ring of
neighbours that separate him from her.

Pacchiarotto, and how he worked in Distemper, although written as one consecutive poem, is, in reality,
composed of two parts.   The first part is an amusing account of a true episode in the life of the painter, Giacomo
Pacchiarotto ; and the second part, under the veil of an
admonition to the same, is an attack from Browning himself upon his critics.   Pacchiarotto lived in the sixteenth
century, and was one of a society called the Bardotti,
whose principal business in life seemed to be to discover
all actual and imaginary abuses, and to suggest innumerable theories for their reform, which they expected other
people to put in practice.   Hence the title, Bardotti,
"spare horses," signifying that they walk quietly beside
the waggon, while others do the labour of drawing it
along.   At last, however, Pacchiarotto discovered that
people were not anxious to be reformed, and that he only
got into trouble by his interference.   He therefore retired for a while from the ungrateful public, and since the
need of hearing his own eloquence was essential to him,
he arranged to give daily orations and sermons in his own
house to an audience which was, at least, silent if not ap-
preciative.   He selected for his purpose a large empty
room, with white-washed walls, on which he painted in
distemper portraits of all sorts and conditions of men,
such as he thought in need of his admonitions, and from
whom he imagined himself receiving suitably deferential
replies and apologies.   This amusement kept him out of
harm's way for a time.   Then famine broke out in Siena,
and the Bardotti once more came to the front with their
advice, which ran as follows :—

"Just substitute servant for master,
    Make Poverty Wealth and Wealth Poverty,
    Unloose Man from overt and covert tie,
    And straight out of social confusion
    True Order would spring!"

To this doctrine the Bardotti were all agreed, until Pacchiarotto suggested himself as the fittest leader in this
new order of things.   Then the whole society turned
upon him with such fury that he was glad to beat an
ignominious retreat, and vanish from their sight as fast as
his heels could carry him.

"Right and left did he dash helter-skelter,
    In agonised search of a shelter,"

which at last he found in a sepulchre.   It was not a
lodging after his taste; but such was his fear of the search
which the "spare horses" might make for the offending
would-be leader, that there he remained for two days.
Then he ventured out, a sadder and a wiser man, and
"gained, in a state past description, a convent of
monks."   This ends the first part.   Then follows the
monk's admonition that the paint-brush, and not social
reform, is Pacchiarotto's business, in which rebuke he
humbly acquiesces.   Lastly, imagining them under the
disguise of a Masque of May-Day chimney-sweeps, who
are aptly accused of bringing with them more dirt than
they find in the chimneys, comes Browning's witty and
good-humoured attack on the criticism of his critics.   In
place of the minute analysis which occurs in most of the
poems, this composition has throughout a boisterous vigour
which goes well with the reckless audacity of the rhymes.

At the Mermaid disclaims the idea that the utterances of the poet necessarily disclose the poet's self, and it also denies that the poet's temperament is essentially sad. Browning considered this last idea a popular fallacy, due in great measure to the influence of Byron. The verses are spoken in the name of Shakespeare, of whom it is certainly more true that the public knows nothing of him but his " work," and is absolutely ignorant as to his inner life, than it is of Browning, who has given us such undeniably personal utterances as the Masque in *Pacchiarotto*, *Prospice*, and the incomparable *One Word More*.

House is also addressed to his indiscriminating critics, and repeats the refusal to exhibit his inner life to the public gaze. But he adds for those whose criticism Browning could really value—

> " Outside should suffice for evidence :
> And whoso desires to penetrate
> Deeper, must dive by the spirit-sense."

In illustration of the wisdom of his refusal, there follows the description of a house from which an earthquake has torn off the front, together with an account of the idle chatter of the neighbours as they rush in to explore the house, indifferent as to the fate of its owner.

Shop is a grave rebuke to such as give their whole lives to nothing but the business of making or trying to make money.

Pisgah-Sights[1] are visions of the truth of life seen by one leaving it. I. is a death-bed vision of life as it is

---

"And Moses went up from the plains of Moab upon the mountain of Nebo, to the top of Pisgah, that is before Jericho."--Deut. xxxiv. 1.

with its apparent hindrances and inconsistencies, and of
the absolute necessity of these.   The pathos of this knowledge, which has come too late, is summed up in the last
words—

> " There's the life lying,
> And I see all of it,
> Only, I'm dying ! "

II. depicts life as it would have been, had such knowledge
shone on the beginning of life instead of on its close, and
we feel that loss, not gain, would have been the result.

Fears and Scruples.—In this poem the speaker protests perfect trust in an unseen friend who has not yet
shown any acknowledgment of the love and trust received.   None the less love and trust remain, and when
friends try to combat the existence of such an unseen
friend, the speaker asks, " What if this friend happen to
be—God ? "

Natural Magic is a tribute to the power of love, which
can clothe with beauty all that was formerly bare and
dreary.   Inexplicable this may be, says the speaker,
" only I feel it."

Magical Nature sings of the beloved, whose beauty is
glorious as that of a flower, unchanging as that of a
jewel.

Bifurcation urges the duty of love to fulfil its mission
of help, and condemns the apparent virtue of sacrificing
love to what seems duty.   Such false sacrifice may bring
content to the one who makes it, but to the other, who
is simply put aside and left to his own devices, it means
ruin.   The poem speaks of such a couple, and implies
that the sinner is not the man who fails from the lack of
love's helping hand, but the woman who refused to lend it.

G

Numpholeptos.[1]—The speaker loves with overwhelming passion a being of another sphere, who, without rejecting his love, requires of him such perfection as no mortal can attain to. Again and again he comes to her, but some flaw is always visible, and he is invariably dismissed to further efforts. Once despair emboldens him, and he breaks out in passionate reproach, but only to be met with the same "sad, slow, silver smile." And he goes forth to try again.

Appearances, a graceful little lyric in two verses, expresses the power of association to beautify what is poor and ugly, or to destroy the beauty of what is almost perfection.

St. Martin's Summer describes a lover who discovers that his lady's charm for him is made up only of the ghost of an older love, which unknowingly he has projected upon her.

Hervé Riel relates the story of the Breton sailor of that name, who, after the battle of La Hogue, guided the French fleet through the narrow passage of the Rance from St. Malo to Solidor, and so saved it from the English, who were in hot pursuit. Simple and strong as the hero of the poem, Hervé Riel is justly one of the most popular of Browning's ballads.

A Forgiveness brings us again to the heights of tragedy. At confession the speaker relates the story of his wife's infidelity, and of the scorn instead of anger which it raised in his heart. For three years they lived together with this silent barrier between them,—he, conscious of her guilt; she, knowing that he knew it. Then his wife confessed the truth. Her infidelity arose from grief and

---

[1] νυμφόληπτος, caught or entranced by a nymph.

despair at his apparent devotion to "state-craft" rather
than to her. Loving him all the time, she had hoped to
win him back by showing him that another valued her
love, if he despised it. Now she saw that all had been
in vain, and she only longed for death to end her misery.
Her confession turned his scorn to hate. He bade her
write her love, and when she offered to do so in her
blood, he handed her a dagger for the purpose. She
wrote, and died that night, for the dagger had been
poisoned. Now, adds the husband,

> " She sleeps, as erst
> Beloved, in this your church; ay, yours!"

And through the grate of the confessional he stabs the
guilty "father."

Cenciaja is connected with Shelley's "The Cenci," in
that it relates an incident which sealed the fate of
Beatrice Cenci when, after long delay, it seemed as if
pardon were at hand. On the very day on which
Beatrice Cenci's fate was to be declared, the Marchesa dell' Oriolo was murdered by her younger son,
Paolo Santa Croce. He escaped, but Beatrice Cenci's
fate for a similar crime was not yet sealed, and " she
shall not flee at least," declared the Pope. The case o
the Marchesa's murder was entrusted to a nephew of the
Pope, Cardinal Aldobrandini. The Cardinal, his public
zeal being whetted, as it afterwards appears, by private
jealousy in a love intrigue, at once arrived at the
conclusion that the elder brother, Onofrio Santa Croce,
would be in Paolo's confidence. Fortune favoured the
Cardinal, for a note from Onofrio of distinctly equivocal
meaning was discovered, on the strength of which he was

arrested and imprisoned. There, "day by day, week by week, and month by month," he was unceasingly ex- amined and cross-examined as to the meaning of the note, until his mind sank into imbecility under the "persistent question-torture," and a false admission of complicity in his mother's death was drawn from him, upon which he was beheaded. The title of the poem, and the proverb which follows it, are best explained in Browning's own words. In a letter to Mr. Buxton Forman, he writes, " ' aia ' is generally an accumulative yet depreciative termination. *Cenciaja—a bundle of rags —a trifle.* The proverb, ' *Agni cencio vuol entrare in bucato,*' means ' every poor creature will be pressing into the company of his betters,' and I used it to deprecate the notion that I intended anything of the kind."

Filippo Baldinucci on the Privilege of Burial: A Reminiscence of A.D. 1676, is a humorous account of an incident recorded in Baldinucci's "History of Painters."

Adjoining the Jewish burial-ground in Florence there was a field belonging to a Christian farmer. In order to annoy the Jews, and under the pretence of protecting his possessions, this farmer engaged a painter, Buti, to paint a picture of the Virgin Mary, which he then fixed so that it overlooked the Jewish cemetery. The Jews resented this, and offered to pay a hundred ducats that the picture should be turned round to face the field. This offer was accepted, and a covered boarding was erected, behind which the alteration was made. When, however, this was completed, the picture of the Virgin Mary certainly no longer faced the cemetery, but in its place there hung a picture of the Crucifixion. At this point (stanza 35) history gives place to fiction. The following morning the farmer and Buti were enjoying a laugh over the discom-

fiture of the Jews, when the door of Buti's shop opened,
and in walked a young Jew of immense stature, with
"a beard that baulks description." Buti quaked with
fear as he recognised the son of the Jewish High Priest,
while the young man with infinite civility explained the
object of his visit. The pictures of Mary and of the
Crucifixion had so struck his fancy that he wished to purchase them for his picture gallery. His "tone so
ominously mild," and "smile terrifically soft," so scared
Buti that he named only just the proper price, and took
the money in abject silence. The farmer, being somewhat bolder, hazarded the suggestion that—

> " Mary in triumph born to deck
>   A Hebrew household,"

implied a miracle, in the Jew's conversion. At this the
Jew straightway made it clear that the only miracle
effected was that which kept his hands off Buti's throat,
and that his conversion consisted in the idea that a
picture of the Virgin Mary may well hang in a gallery
together with other works of art. With this explanation
he shouldered his purchase, and walked off. The farmer
tells the tale to his little son to show why he must not
pelt Jews.

Epilogue is a powerful attack on the freely-expressed
view that Browning's poetry is stiff reading. The position which he takes is substantially that those who complain of a lack in him of that grace which, as they al-
lege, they find in classical English poets, have not read
even the Masters whom they pretend, for fashion's sake, to
admire. The poem opens with a line from Mrs. Browning,—"The poets pour us wine"—and then proceeds to

compare wine and poetry, and to analyse the ingredients necessary to both. Strength and sweetness in both can only be blended to a ꞏꞏ ꞏderate extent, and this does not satisfy the public. The complaints at lack of sweetness are, however, not genuine. Shakespeare and Milton are admitted food for all, yet in the cellars of the general public

> " There are
> Forty barrels with Shakespeare's brand ;
> Some five or six are abroach ; "

while from Milton " mere drippings suffice." These being thus neglected, Browning boldly declares the essence of his work and vintage—

> " Man's thoughts, and loves, and hates !
> Earth is my vineyard—these grew there :
> From grape of the ground, I made or marred
> My vintage ; easy the task or hard,
> Who set it—His praise be my reward."

La Saisiaz, 1878, is one of the few poems in which Browning acknowledges his own personality in the views and sentiments expressed. It is Browning and no one else who speaks here ; Browning, whose faith has never failed him indeed, but who now suddenly feels the need of again convincing himself that it is no myth, but a Divine reality, that death is not the "ending once and always." The need for his own satisfaction of thus once more defining the tenets of his faith, arose from the shock of the sudden death of a dear friend, Miss Anne Egerton Smith, who had been staying with him and his sister at a villa called La Saisiaz, near Geneva. The poem commences with a reminiscence

of how the speaker reached the summit of a certain
hill alone, which only the night before he had planned
to climb with her who had been taken away. He
speaks of the commonplace leave they took of each
other, with no foreboding of the long parting which was
before them. The next morning, after his usual bathe,
he returned expecting to meet his friend ready for the ex-
pedition, and he describes his horror at finding her
dead. As he stood on the summit, where she should
have been by his side, he was meditating and seeking a
reason for her being so suddenly taken away. He endeavoured to console himself with the thought that she
was happier there than here, when the question suddenly
flashed through his mind, "Is there in truth an after-
life?" The doubt shook him for a moment, but he would
not shirk it. There and then he faced the question and
bravely answered it. Giving play alternately to Reason
and Fancy, he comes ultimately to the knowledge that
he himself possesses an invincible hope of future life, a
hope so strong that it may fairly be described as expectation.

The Two Poets of Croisic,[1] 1878.—The poem tells
two tales showing the little worth of fame ; and the Prologue and Epilogue, as well as some incidental verses in
the body of the poem, suggest love as the one thing need-
ful either with it or without it.

The poem itself opens by the fireside, round which
husband and wife sit watching the blazing logs.
The logs are of ship timber,[2] in which the husband
easily conjures up a ship which quickly bears him within
sight of Croisic and of the strange, Druid-like worship

---

[1] Published with *La Saisiaz*.
[2] Cf. *James Lee's Wife*.

which still holds sway there, despite the progress of
civilisation. But Druid, Christian, or Jew, men differ
much, no doubt, but resemble each other more.   So without further prelude our poets step upon the scene, different
in many ways, with a century between them, but alike in
that each enjoyed

> " Such a mighty moment of success
> As pinnacled him straight, in full display
> For the whole world to worship."

Since when their very names would long since have been
forgotten were it not for Piron's " Metronamie " and
Browning's poems.

The first poet, René Gentilhomme, was by occupation
page to the Prince of Condé, who, by reason of Louis XIII.
being childless, was regarded as the future king of France,
and openly styled "now Duke; next King." All his
leisure René spent in verse-making. One day, while he
was busily employed with an ode on Love, a thunderstorm
broke out, and the lightning struck and destroyed the
Duke's crown, which a moment before had been safe on
a marble pillar close by where René was sitting. The
incident flashed upon René as a revelation, and forthwith
he turned his ode into a prophecy that, as surely as the
lightning had destroyed the Duke's crown, so surely were
his hopes of succeeding to the throne also dashed to the
ground. Before the next year dawned a dauphin would
be born, and Condé plain duke again. The prophecy
proved true, and René was appointed Court poet to Louis
XIII. But this first success proved also his last. He
wrote nothing afterwards worthy of the name of poetry,
and sank completely into insignificance. Browning

imagines that, believing certainly that God had directly dealt with him, René found

> " That, after prophecy, the rhyming-trick
> Is poor employment : human praises scare
> Rather than soothe ears all a-tingle yet
> With tones few hear and live, but none forget. "

The second poet, Paul Desforges Maillard, has a more interesting and more amusing, if equally transitory, experience of success. For many years, to his great chagrin, his poems were continually rejected more or less politely by every journal to which he sent them. At last his sister came to the rescue. Copying some of the weakest of her brother's verses, she sent them with a humble little note, begging his opinion on her first efforts, to the very editor who had rejected them. Not recognising the verses under the alleged authorship of Mdlle. Malcrais de la Vigne, the editor enthusiastically accepted them. More verses, equally bad, followed with equal success, and at length the editor and Voltaire himself were at her feet. Believing that his worth was at last recognised, and refusing to credit that it was the lady's name that had worked the change, Paul set off for Paris to receive the honours now acknowledged his due. His reception, when he made himself known to the editor and Voltaire, was not all he could have desired. Nevertheless he felt confident that " the world could not eat its own printed words, and that the poems it had so praised must now succeed." They failed, however, and his imagined glory vanished like a flash o light.

The delicacy and tenderness of the Prologue and Epilogue make them conspicuous in the poem. The Prologue shows all things cold, dark, and sordid, till love shines on them. The Epilogue tells a little tale of one who was singing for a prize to the accompaniment of his lyre. A string snapped ; but before the harmony could fail, a cricket perched on the lyre, and sang the missing notes till the end of the song. That, says Browning, is what a girl's love does.

XV.—DRAMATIC IDYLLS (1879). In these poems Browning deals almost for the first time with the poor. The interest of each poem also depends more on action than is usual with him.

Martin Relph depicts with painful realism the life-long remorse and agony caused by a moment's hesitation and lack of moral courage. The speaker is apparently a young man, who has heard from his grandfather the story which he relates in Martin Relph's own words. When little more than a boy, Martin Relph had been present at the execution of a young woman who was sus-pected of being a spy. As the fatal signal was given, the bystanders hid their faces. He alone gazed at the scene, and saw in the distance a man rushing wildly on, waving a paper above his head. The truth flashed into his mind at once. It was Vincent Parkes, the girl's lover, bearing the proofs of her innocence. Whether from frantic jealousy because he loved the girl himself, or simply from boyish terror, Martin Relph can never determine, but he stood there for a moment paralysed and speechless. The next moment it was too late. Rosa-mund Page had fallen under the guns, and at the sight Vincent Parkes dropped dead. Ever since that terrible day Martin Relph has been a prey to remorse, and he strives to silence the strings of conscience by yearly confession of his cowardice upon the spot where the tragedy had taken place.

Pheidippides relates the Greek legend of how Phei-dippides, the runner, was sent to seek from Sparta help for Athens against Persia. Pheidippides describes his journey with picturesque vividness, and tells how, re-turning from a fruitless mission, he met the goat-god Pan, who promised, not alone to assist Athens, but to reward him for his zeal. This reward, he imagined, would be release from his office as runner, and prosperity in the home he should then make with the woman he loved. So far Pheidippides speaks. An eye-witness completes the tale. After the battle of Marathon was won, Phei-dippides was sent to announce the victory at Athens. As he reached Athens, he cried out, "Rejoice, we con-quer !" and, exhausted, fell dead in his glory.

Halbert and Hob relates the extraordinary effect of a sudden flash of moral consciousness upon two men, until then

" Harsh and fierce of word, rough and savage of deed."

They were father and son, and lived together in one incessant war of words and blows. One Christmas night, after a quarrel more fierce than usual, Halbert rose, and seizing his father by the throat, was on the point of flinging him from the hut into the bitter winter night outside. Suddenly the old man's struggles ceased, and passively he let his son drag him to the door. Then he spoke. Years before, he said, he had treated his father as Halbert now treated him ; but at the door, a better self had prevailed and he had stopped in time. Let Halbert now do likewise. At his words, Halbert

loosed his hold, and in silence they re-entered the room
together. In silence they passed the night. The next
morning Hob sat there dead, while Halbert crouched
trembling on the ground, an idiot.

The poem ends with the quotation from Shakespeare's
King Lear,

"Is there a reason in Nature for these hard hearts?"

to which Browning answers,

"That a reason out of Nature must turn them soft,
　　seems clear!"

Iván Ivànovitch is an account, terrible in its intensity
and realism, of an incident supposed to have occurred in
Russia. A woman travelling with her three children
through the forest was attacked by wolves. Fear and
the instinct of self-preservation were stronger than the
mother's love, and in an agony of terror she let the wolves
seize one after another of her children. She alone escaped,
and arrived at her native village half dead with grief and
fear. A friend, Iván Ivànovitch, the village carpenter,
greeted and soothed her till she recovered, and could tell
her tale. At its close Iván spoke no word, but, as she
lay there prostrate, he raised his axe, and severed her
head from her body. Then he spoke,

"It had to be:
I could no other: God it was bade 'act for me.'"

Very soon the whole village was in commotion, and
Iván Ivànovitch was tried for murder. Some praised,
some blamed the deed; but at the end of the trial the

aged Pope, whose word was law, proclaimed "Ivàn Ivànovitch, God's servant." A bystander carried him news of his acquittal, and found him kneeling on the floor, playing with his children.

> "They told him he was free
> As air, to walk abroad. 'How otherwise?' asked he."

Such is the tale, but words are utterly inadequate to describe the power with which it is told. The mother's agony of mind during the terrible drive is told with many a break and pause in the verse. And this lends additional force to the change of metre at the description of the moment when the wolves have almost overtaken the sledge. The sudden change at this point to anapæsts suggests the regular gallop of the pack of wolves with painful realism.

Tray is an idyll of less tragic interest, in which Browning derides the usually accepted type of hero, and he illustrates his scorn by the following true and simple story. A child in Paris fell in the water; while the bystanders stood stupefied and motionless, a dog plunged into the river, and rescued first the child and then her doll, after which he trotted quietly off, unconscious of his glory. With indignant sarcasm [1] Browning relates that an onlooker wished to buy and vivisect that dog so that,—

> "At expense
> Of half-an-hour and eighteenpence,
> How brain secretes dog's soul, we'll see !"

Ned Bratts.—With regard to this poem Browning wrote, "The story of old Tod, as told in Bunyan's 'Life

---

[1] Cf. *Arcades Ambo. Asolando.*

and Death of Mr. Badman,' was distinctly in my mind when I wrote *Ned Bratts* at the Splugen, without reference to what I had read when quite a boy." From remarks which Browning made to Dr. Furnivall on the subject of this first series of DRAMATIC IDYLLS, it is evident that he himself considered *Ned Bratts* the best poem in the volume. It is, however, by no means the most pleasant, although undoubtedly it is extremely powerful. It deals with the conversion of Ned Bratts and his wife, who voluntarily deliver themselves over to justice, and indeed implore that in order that their souls may be saved hereafter, they may now be hanged, as they so richly deserve.

DRAMATIC IDYLLS, Second Series (1880).

Echetlos, like *Pheidippides*, is a tale of the battle of Marathon. It tells of the unknown hero who in the disguise of a "clown" ploughed the field of Marathon to such good effect that he effectually rooted up the living weeds (Medes and Persians), and saved the day and the glory of Greece. Then silently he vanished, and the oracle bade the Greeks leave his name enshrouded in mystery, since "the great deed ne'er grows small;" whereas a great name sometimes does.

Clive.—The anecdote which this poem relates was told to Browning by Mrs. Jameson, a fortnight after she had heard it from Lord Macaulay. Browning has reproduced the exact details of the story, but has added slightly thereto, in accordance with his own conception of Clive's character. The poem is in the form of a monologue, spoken by an old comrade, who tells the tale exactly as Clive himself had told it to him a fortnight before his suicide. The subject is a duel which Clive fought at the age of fifteen with an officer whom he had accused

of cheating at cards. With inexperienced hand, Clive
fired too soon, and to no purpose; whereupon the officer
held his loaded pistol to the lad's head, and dared him to
repeat his accusation. Boldly, without flinching, he re-
peated the charge, and the officer, impressed by his courage, and confounded by his own guilty conscience,
threw down the pistol, owned his guilt, and rushed from
the room. The bystanders vowed vengeance on him;
but Clive scornfully declared that not one of them had
interfered to save his life, and therefore now he would
challenge whichever of them spoke a word against the
honour of the man who had spared him.

Clive had related the incident in response to his friend's
inquiry, "When were you most brave?" and in order
to illustrate his own enigmatical answer, "The time I
felt most fear." But, he explains, (and it is here that
Browning draws upon his imagination simply), it was not
death at the hand of his enemy which he feared, but
rather contemptuous mercy, arising from assumed pity of
his youth and inexperience. Such mercy from a cheat
and bully would have left him no alternative but to
"pick his weapon up, and use it on myself."

Muléykeh, an old Arabian story, is by far the most
beautiful of these later idylls. Hoseyn was the owner
of Muleykeh the Pearl, the finest and swiftest horse
in the country; and though he had little else to call
his own, this possession made him the happiest and
most contented of men. Duhl, the son of Sheyban,
sought in vain to buy his treasure, and at last came
craftily by night, and stole Muléykeh. Hoseyn, who
slept in the stable, soon missed her, and at once gave
chase. He rapidly gained upon the thief, for the Pearl,
missing the accustomed "tap of the heel, the touch

of the bit," did not exert her usual speed. But, just as he came within reach of his darling, the thought struck Hoseyn that to overtake her would be to own her beaten in the race. Unselfish love and pride conquered, and in despair he cried aloud the secret of her unrivalled speed. Duhl was wise at the word, and Muléykeh, re- cognising her master's voice, bounded away beyond all reach of recapture. Weeping, Hoseyn returned home, and told his story. Friends and neighbours laughed at him for his folly in actually aiding the thief, when by a moment's silence and haste he would have regained Muléykeh.

" ' And the beaten in speed,' wept Hoseyn ; ' you never have loved my Pearl.' "

This line, and Guido's frantic cry, "Pompilia, will you let them murder me ? "[1] have been quoted by Professor Westcott as the two finest lines Browning ever wrote, and which, he declares, no one but Browning could have written. They go to the very depths of the two men's hearts.

Pietro of Albano derives its title from the Italian philo- sopher and physician, Petrus Aponensis, who flourished in the thirteenth century ; but it seems that the legend which Browning has applied to Pietro is an old popular fiction, which has been told in turn of various other per- sons. The tale is of a magician who earns a precarious living by the use of the highest magical skill, gaining when successful only a jealous reproach for meddling with the black arts.

---

[1] *Ring and Book*, vol. iv., line 2427.

Doctor—relates a legend from the Talmud, in illustration of the saying that "A bad wife is stronger than Death or Satan."

Pan and Luna repeats Virgil's legend of the capture of the moon by Pan. Ashamed at her own uncovered beauty, she sought the shelter of some clouds, behind which lurked Pan, her betrayer, who had set them as a trap. Since then she never remains behind a cloud longer than is necessary to break through it. And Browning asks, "No lesson for a maid leaves she?"

The DRAMATIC IDYLLS, Second Series (1880), contain also two short poems without title, as *Prologue* and *Epilogue* respectively. The former verses contrast the doubts and ignorance admitted in respect to the body with the certainty and wisdom pretended in respect to man's soul. The latter verses express Browning's view that the great poet's nature is not a fertile soil on which every flower-seed blossoms, but a rock from whose cleft grows slowly the abiding pine.

JOCOSERIA, 1883.—This volume (as its name suggests) includes a wide variety of subjects, which may almost be said to range from the sublime to the ridiculous.

It begins with a short poem without title, telling how, in the complete incompleteness of summer with its blue sky and roses and green leaves, there is wanting for perfection only love.

Donald is a true story, which was related to Browning by the so-called Donald himself. The motive of the poem is obviously to censure the instinctive brutality which love of sport engenders, just as in *Tray* Browning censures the idle curiosity which seeks useless and merely barbaric vivisection.

A sportsman, passing along a narrow ledge of rock

H

above a precipice, was suddenly confronted by a fine stag, who barred further passage. It was an impossibility for the two to pass each other; and it was evident that, unless he made way for the animal, or went back, the stag would thrust him over the precipice. The man therefore lay down flat upon the ledge, and the stag at once, with the utmost caution, began to step over him. At the sight of the beauty of the animal, however, the sportsman's instinct within him asserted itself, and he stabbed the stag. Together they rolled over on to the rocks below, the dying stag falling undermost, thus again saving the man from death. But his injuries were severe, and on his recovery he was an utter cripple, only able to gain his livelihood by crawling from tavern to tavern, where the recital of his tale generally earned him a few pence. And, adds Browning, "rightly rewarded, ingrate."

Solomon and Balkis relates an amusing legend from the Talmud concerning the visit of the Queen of Sheba to Solomon. Solomon and the queen for some time deceive each other with fine talk—he declaring that in the company of the wise alone can he find pleasure, she that her joy is only in the company of the good—when suddenly upon Balkis' finger the king sees

> " The Ring which bore the Name . . .
>   The truth-compelling Name ! "

Then each drops the mask and owns the truth. Solomon, that he welcomes the wise, provided always that they extol him ; Balkis, that she delights in the company of the good,

" Provided the good are the young, men strong and tall
    and proper."

And her object in coming so far to visit the king has been

                    " Sage Solomon—
    One fool's small kiss ! "

Cristina and Monaldeschi presents a powerful sketch
of a woman's vengeance. The speaker is Queen Cristina of
Sweden, who with Count Monaldeschi is pacing a corri-
dor in the palace at Fontainebleau. With bitter taunts and
scathing sarcasm she shows him how fully she is aware of
his treachery. Illustrating her words by metaphors suggested by the tapestry on the walls, she reveals to Monaldeschi
his danger and utter helplessness, and mockingly suggests
that the danger might be averted, would he but crouch at
her feet again, and seem to love her as before. But with
every word she utters she is leading him nearer and
nearer to his doom. In the " Chamber of the Fawn " she
has stationed a priest who is to confess him and the
soldiers who are to murder him, while she looks on un-
moved at the ghastly spectacle. The fierce cruelty with
which she plays with her cowardly victim and gloats
over his agony are portrayed with striking if painful
realism. The final moral left on the reader's mind, however, is much the same as that with which *Donald* ends.

Mary Wollstonecraft and Fuseli is a woman's patient
but passionate lament of an unrequited love. There is
little reason to believe that the poem is founded upon
fact.

Adam, Lilith and Eve.—Adam is sitting with Lilith,
the woman who had loved him, and Eve, the wife who had

sometime loved another. The love of the one and the indifference of the other for Adam had alike been concealed, until the terror of a thunderstorm suddenly impels each to speak, and confess the truth as to her past feelings. The storm once over, each sees her imprudence clearly, and, with a laugh, pretends she had only been in joke. The husband, too stupid to see that in their terror they had spoken truth, replies, "I saw through the joke," and the old life goes on as before.

Ixion.—Suiting the subject, the verse is unrhymed hexameters and pentameters of remarkable strength and ease.

Ixion speaks from the burning wheel to which he is chained. He relates his story, and declares his punishment, as well as Zeus who inflicted it, to be unjust. It is this sense of injustice which first convinces him that Zeus cannot be the highest power. Zeus knew that Ixion sinned in ignorance, and yet punished him ; and therefore Zeus must be less than man, not more. Out of the wreck which Zeus has made, Ixion declares that he rises "past Zeus, to the Potency o'er him."

Jochanan Hakkadosh (John the Holy).—This poem purports to be derived from a Talmudic writing, the title of which is, "A Collection of Many Lies." [1]

It records the supposed prolongation of the life of John

---

[1] This title is, of course, pure invention. With regard to the alleged superstition concerning the prolongation of life by the sacrifice of part of the life of another, there is a legend about Adam to whom life was granted for one day (= 1,000 years); but when, on reviewing the coming generations, he noticed the youngest son of Jesse being deprived of life altogether, he prayed to God to take 70 years of his (Adam's) life, and give them to the son of Jesse (David). Thence Adam lived 930 years : David. 70.

the Holy by his pupils, who each sacrificed a certain period of his own life to lengthen that of the Rabbi. John tells the experiences which that period has brought him, and in no one of them finds content. But in a final extension of life which, unknown to his friends, had been sacrificed for him by some boy, or had been permitted by God, he tells how he has learnt the unspeakable secret of life's mystery, and in utter happiness he dies.

Never the Time and the Place is one of the most beautiful of the love songs.

> " Never the time and the place,
> And the loved one all together ! "

sings the poet, but "time" and "place" are of no account, and the "loved one" is all that is needed.

Pambo relates a true story of a certain foolish person of that name, who is said to have spent many years in studying the verse (Psalm xxxix.),

> "I said, I will look to my ways
> That I with my tongue offend not."

The first line was easy to act upon, but Pambo was baffled by the second. The last verse serves as a sort of epilogue, and is addressed to Browning's critics With good-humoured mock modesty he admits that,

> " I keep my sunrise Aim
>
>   .   .   .   .
>
> And *look to my ways*, yet much the same,
> *Offend with my tongue*—like Pambo."

XVI.—FERISHTAH'S FANCIES (1884). Concerning

this volume Browning wrote in a letter to a friend:—
"*Above all, pray allow for the poet's inventiveness in
any case, and do not suppose there is more than a thin
disguise of a few Persian names and illusions. There
was no such person as Ferishtah—the stories are all in-
ventions. . . . The Hebrew quotations are put in for a
purpose, as a direct acknowledgment that certain doc-
trines may be found in the Old Book, which the Con-
cocters of Novel Schemes of Morality put forth as
discoveries of their own.*" From this, as well as from
the quotation from King Lear[1] at the beginning of the
volume, we may gather that it is Browning himself who
speaks through the disguise of Ferishtah. The volume
consists of twelve *Fancies*, a *Prologue*, and *Epilogue*.

The Prologue is fanciful in the extreme, illustrating
the method of the whole collection of fancies by a
humorous description of a certain famous Italian dish, in
which various ingredients, unpalatable alone, combine to
yield their proper flavour. Each fancy is followed by a
lyric bearing upon almost the same subject, but mostly in
the form of a love-song, one more delicate and beautiful
than another.

I. *The Eagle* tells how the desire to become a dervish
and to minister to his fellow-men first entered the heart
of Ferishtah. With this desire came the knowledge that,
in order to teach, he must first learn; and to this end
Ferishtah determined that he would leave the woods in
which the desire to help mankind had come to him, and
so live among men that he might learn their deepest

---

[1] "You, sir, I entertain for one of my hundred; only I do not like
the fashion of your garments; you will say they are Persian; but let
them be changed."

needs, and afterwards endeavour to supply them. The lyric which follows condemns the selfishness which makes two lovers live for each other only, and declares that true love should the better enable those who are so blessed to help their fellow-men.

II. *The Melon-Seller* shows the second lesson which Ferishtah learnt before he became a dervish, and which may be summed up in the last two lines of the poem—

> " Shall we receive good at the hand of God,
>   And evil not receive,"

The lyric declares that, should the loved one be for once unjust, yet the memory of how often she has lavished upon him more than his deserts may well teach her lover to suffer once with patience.

III. *Shah Abbas* presents the first lesson which Ferishtah teaches after he has become a dervish. It declares God weighs and values faith and faith according to the way in which it is endured by the heart, not according to the accuracy with which it is deduced by the head. The lyric speaks of love as the light, and of trust as the guide, with which the heart of the loved one should be explored.

IV. *The Family* opens the question as to whether prayer does not in some cases imply want of faith in the wisdom of the Almighty. It may seem so, admits Ferishtah ; but not to pray for those we love argues us either more or less than man, which is not good. Our place in the world is that of man and nothing more.

> " Man, who as man conceiving, hopes and fears,
>   And craves and deprecates, and loves and loathes,

> And bids God help him, till death touch his eyes,
> And show God granted most, denying all."

The lyric repeats the assertion that man is human, not divine, and the speaker adds that it is best so.

V. *The Sun* is in defence of that worship which can only conceive the idea of the Deity in a human form. Man, argues Ferishtah, can understand only that which he himself can experience ; therefore the idea of humanity in the Deity is justifiable and free from blame. Love and gratitude are the highest attributes of worship ; and these man can only offer in the mere human way in which he has felt them. To do this as best he can is his duty ; and it is right to respect any man doing this, however little one can understand his faith. The lyric speaks of how, in the glory and splendour of fire, its birth in the humble flint is quite forgotten or ignored.

VI. *Mihrab Shah* illustrates the view that

> " Put pain from out the world, what room were left
> For thanks to God for love to man ? "

In the lyric the speaker compares his own physical strength and mental sloth with the bodily weakness and active mind of his wife, and suggests that, being thus handicapped, they may keep the closer together.

VII. *A Camel Driver* condemns the equal punishment of faults committed deliberately and those done in ignorance. Faults of ignorance often punish themselves, but at any rate deserve neither blame nor forgiveness. In the recognition of this fact lies the distinction between God's judgment and that of man. The lyric also treats of the fallibility of human judgment.

VIII. *Two Camels* exposes the folly of those who exercise undue vigour in neglecting the good things of this

world, thinking thereby to grow wise. "How," asks
Ferishtah, "can mind or body grow strong, and bear the
burden of life bravely to the end, if nourished only on dry
husks? and how can man teach the due use and value of
joy in the world, if not from his own experience? Therefore, desire joy, and thank God for it." The lyric deals
with the idea that from the joys of earth we may conceive
what Heaven may be. This suggestion is illustrated,
first by the description of a chemical experiment, and then
more poetically by reference to the heaven of love.

IX. *Cherries* dwells upon the fact that a gift is rightly
valued not for its intrinsic worth, but for the spirit in
which it is given; a trifle which loving thought has prepared being of more value than gold or jewels carelessly
bestowed. The lyric speaks of life as too short a period
in which to extract all the wealth which "verse-making"
should yield; but, "I said, 'To do little is bad, to do
nothing is worse,' and made verse." With love-making,
he says, the matter is different; for love has no need of
time, but exists here and hereafter.

X. *Plot Culture* propounds the question as to how far
man is a free agent, and responsible for his own life.
Ferishtah replies that, as the gardener of an estate is
practically master of the plot under his charge, and yet
is responsible for it to his employer, so man is master of
his own life, yet at Judgment Day he will be accountable
to God for the use he has made of it. The lyric as usual
leads the same idea into the region of love, where the
speaker urges that sense and soul must unite, and each
complete the other.

XI. *A Pillar at Sebzevah* argues that love is worth infinitely more than knowledge. What one learns to-day,
says Ferishtah, is useless to-morrow, being replaced by

something better; and this incessant change with its inevitable sense of disappointment goes on, whereas love
is unchangeable, and lives forever. In illustration of
the superiority of love over knowledge, Ferishtah speaks
of a certain sun-dial near Sebzevah. Should the towns-
men, he asks, seek to know the motive of the man who
placed it there for their convenience, before they feel due
love, in this case gratitude, that there it is? Thus he ends,
love God, rather than pretend to know Him. The lyric
counsels silent love which shall be felt, not spoken.

XII. *A Bean-Stripe: also Apple-Eating*, is an eloquent
and discursive answer to the question, "Is life good or
bad?" Life, says Ferishtah, holds both good and evil,
black and white; and the shadow of evil falls upon the
good, and tinges it with sadness, while the brightness of
good shines upon the evil. Thus the two extremes meet
and blend, forming neither black nor white entirely,
but what may be symbolised as grey. Life cannot
stagnate; for good or evil it must progress continually,
and the past and future shed alternate light and darkness
upon the present, making it grey or dim of hue according
to the nature of each individual, and to his power of
looking upon the bright side of things. That is the moral
illustrated by the *Bean-Stripe;* and for that which is
good, even as for the sweetness in an apple, not the thing
itself, but God who gave it, is to be thanked. The lyric
asserts that justice, not love, is all that is due from the
world to Ferishtah's work, since his motive was to achieve
an ideal found not in the world, but beyond it.

The *Epilogue* presents a view of life here and hereafter,
when the joys of Eternity shall replace earth's pain and
sorrow. The speaker is surrounded by love and happiness, and his words are of passionate love, ending with

the suggestion that the glory he has portrayed may be only the reflection of his own happiness. But it seems as if that would content him.

PARLEYINGS WITH CERTAIN PEOPLE OF IMPORTANCE IN THEIR DAY (1887).—Throughout this group of poems, no less than in Ferishtah's Fancies, the personality of Browning himself is evident. From the Prologue, "Apollo and the Fates," to the Epilogue, "Fust and his Friends," two sketches in entirely different styles, his identity is unmistakable. Repeatedly there are plainly visible below the surface of the legend the foundation stones of his estimate of life—1st., that uncertainty is necessary to spiritual progress; 2nd., that the necessity for the existence of evil must be admitted in the scheme of creation; and, lastly, that faith, hope, and love form the pathway which leads to God.

Apollo and the Fates relates the story of how Apollo, the god of the Sun, descended into Hades to intercede with the Fates for the life of Admetus, who was threatened with an early death. Unsuccessful at first in his errand, Apollo persuades the three sisters to taste the wine which he has brought; and he promises to show them that, although it may be, as they say, that mortal happiness is only an illusion, yet man has the power of continually creating that illusion, and need therefore never wake to the knowledge of its unreality. Under the influence of the wine, Atropos, who was about to cut the thread of Admetus' life, consents to spare him, and with delirious joy the Fates break into song and dancing. Suddenly an explosion from the centre of the earth sobers them. In fear and humility they recognise the anger of Zeus, their Omnipotent, that each has sought to leave the place assigned to her, and to assume the function of a higher Power. It is not the duty of the Fates to pronounce sentence of life or death, but to execute. It is Apollo's duty to encourage faith and hope throughout life, not to place a limit upon these by certainty of knowledge. In keeping with this dogma of uncertainty is the compromise which the sisters now make concerning Admetus. He shall live, they say, should there be found someone else willing to die for him. Apollo asserts that there will be many ready to sacrifice themselves for their king, but that Admetus will choose death. Here, with the derisive laughter of the Fates at Apollo's simple faith, the prologue ends.

Bernard de Mandeville, the first of the group of chosen spirits with whom Browning holds commune in his parleying, was a Dutch physician at the end of the last century, who, however, practised in England as soon as he had taken his degree. He was the author of "The Fable of the Bees," and also of several medical works. The help which Browning claims from Bernard de Mandeville is, as he says, "no fresh knowledge," but the power to disprove certain pessimistic arguments (in which we can plainly trace Carlyle), and to establish indisputably the advantage to be gained by gratefully accepting the existence of an all-powerful Love to encourage us on our way, instead of cavilling at the existence of sin and evil.

Daniel Bartoli forms a contrast, and a delightful one, to its predecessor. Although we feel the truth of Browning's arguments in *Bernard de Mandeville,* and in spite of the undeniable charm in the measured swing of the verse, yet to many it must undoubtedly seem dry reading. *Daniel Bartoli* is written in musical rhyme, the echo

of which lingers pleasantly in our ears.   The story
which Browning chooses from Bartoli's chronicles is
that of Duke Charles IV. of Lorraine, who fell in love
with Marianne Pagot, a chemist's daughter. Duke Charles
had previously agreed to sign a deed of gift, making over
certain of his lands to the king, Louis XIV., who, fearing
that on his marriage Charles would seek to cancel the
deed, grants his consent solely on condition that the
original agreement should be adhered to.   This message
was delivered to the lady, who indignantly bade the
Duke destroy the agreement and relinquish all hope of
court favour, rather than relinquish lands with which God
had endowed him in trust only.   Charles, however, had
not the courage, and Marianne left him. After some
years she married the Marquis de Lassay, who, although
a mere child at the time, had been deeply impressed by
her conduct.   Their married life was extremely happy,
but of brief duration, for Marianne died.   As for the
Duke, Browning pictures him as leading a frivolous
life, in which he declares that it is his ghost which
walks earth now, whilst his real self lies hidden, waiting
to rise at the call of his first and only true love.   Thus
does Browning vindicate the power of love and faith.
Though weakness has spoilt their beauty, yet it is power-
less to utterly destroy them.

In *Christopher Smart*, Browning calls upon Smart to
explain why, having such rare gift of poetry as he displayed
in "A Song of David," he afterwards neglected poetry
for prose?   He illustrates by a simile his reproof at
the fact that the flash of genius which produced "A Song
of David" was the first and last.   He describes a dream,
in which he imagines himself to be exploring a large
empty house, in which he finds everywhere evidence of

moderate wealth and moderate taste. Suddenly, however, he comes upon a room which is fitted up as a
chapel, and in which he finds everything that ancient
and modern art could show. Magnificence and beauty
reign throughout the apartment; but on leaving it he finds
the remaining rooms as mediocre and commonplace as
before. And for the moment Christopher Smart represents in Browning's eyes just such a house ; but, consider
the matter as he will, he can find no satisfactory explanation for the poetic fire which flared up so brightly once
and once only, and that during the period of Smart's
insanity. He finds, however, cause for praise in that at
least Smart has not followed the fashion of the day by
beginning at what should rightly be the end of our
knowledge. He has at least proved his belief that—

> " Live and learn,
> Not first learn, and then live is our concern."

George Bubb Dodington, the subject of this *Parleying*,
was a disreputable politician in the reign of George I.;
and Browning explains to him by what errors he con-
trived to fail in the career which he had chosen. For
the purposes of argument he assumes that self-interest,
and, in pursuance thereof, humbug, are legitimate and
even praiseworthy. The only disgrace is to be found out.
" If, therefore, you cannot be an honest politician," says
Browning, " you should at least be a successful one, and
you will never succeed in gaining followers unless you
can inspire men with a belief that your powers are in
some way superior to their own. Men will not submit
to their equals. Formerly superior physical force gained
men power ; then intelligence and wit held sway ; or,

failing these, mere simple cunning replaced them. A man smilingly professed his aims to be the good of mankind, and he was believed until he was found out. But now such deception is grown too common, and men can only be ruled by belief in the supernatural, because that involves something which is not apparent. Therefore, first arrogating to yourself powers superior to those of all men, except a select few, of whom everyone will think himself one, gain their attention; then, by professing that such arrogance was a mere blind to your own very low opinion of yourself, you shall make them believe that you are really a man of exceptional gifts. But," says Browning, " as you missed this secret, you are known as just a fool and a knave."

The " parleying " with *Francis Furini* deals with a defence of painting and sculpture from the nude, and begins with Browning's emphatic refusal to believe that Furini, as had been alleged, regretted having followed that line of art, or that on his death-bed he desired that all such of his pictures should be destroyed. To foul minds, says he, such art may suggest foul thoughts ; but one might for that reason as well deprive one's self of the pure delight which such pictures give to the pure, as not wear gems because thieves long to steal them. This presentation of the nude, properly considered, is only a special case of the painter's duty to express through form the soul of man, and therefore to depict the body which the soul permeates. Great stress is laid on the fact that such painting is the antithesis to the materialism of evolution, in which, if soul is reached at all, it is by a physical development from matter. To Furini, on the contrary, the soul is the one certainty, and his art is to use the body as a medium for showing it.

Gerard de Lairesse, a Dutch painter of the latter end
of the seventeenth century, was struck blind at the age of
fifty.   While still a child, Browning had come across
a work which he dictated after his blindness, and had been
highly delighted with it.   The portion of it entitled
"The Walk" most struck his fancy, in which the most
commonplace surroundings are made by imagination to
yield interest.   To illustrate de Lairesse's power of ob-
servation, Browning tells us how, finding an empty
sepulchre with a thunderbolt carved upon the lid, Gerard
de Lairesse at once jumped to the conclusion that the
sepulchre represented Phaeton's tomb, while a piece of a
broken wheel half buried in the sand served to furnish in
his imagination the "Chariot of the Sun." Browning
then proceeds to discuss whether modern imagination is
weaker than ancient, taking in this case poetry as the
medium of expression, and stating as his position that,

> "If we no longer see as you of old,
>   'Tis we see deeper   .   .   .
>   .   .   .   .
>   You saw the body, 'tis the soul we see."

None the less, Browning declares, hand in hand with
this new, nobler insight of the soul, there walks the old,
vivid imagination, and in order to prove his words, he
challenges Gerard de Lairesse to once more tread the
"Walk" with him.   Thereupon follows a wonderful
word-painting, which proves incontestably the power of
imagination in at least one poet of the nineteenth century.
The subjects Browning chooses for his picture are the
earth and sky in the various aspects they assume during a
day from early morning until night.   A storm rages at

dawn, and by the lightning flashes may be seen Prometheus chained to his rock, the vulture cowering at his feet. At break of day, when Nature shakes off the stupor of the night, there appears through the glories of the newly risen sun Artemis, pure, cold, and cruel, goddess of sudden death, the huntress-queen. Noon, with its burning heat, brings before us shady nooks in which we find Lyda and the Satyr once more repeating the piteous story of despised love. Sunset, the hour of expectation between the close of the day and the beginning of the night, shows us the silent preparations for approaching battle between the kings Darius and Alexander. And when day is past and night has settled over the face of the earth, all that is left is a shadow, a ghost holding out deprecating hands towards the vanishing past, but power-less to strive towards the future. Here Browning ceases his pictures, and proceeds to contrast the cheerless view of life bred by the old Greek Hades-doctrine with the brightness which should be derived from our modern view that "what once lives never dies;" winding up with a few cheerful words on Spring in illustration of his meaning. This part of his contention is perhaps more characteristic of Browning than of his time.

With *Charles Avison*, a Newcastle composer of the early time of the Georges, Browning assumes an attitude half critical, half explanatory. His aim is to interpret the power and effect of music on the soul of man ; but, before attempting this, he relates the very simple cause which had led his thoughts into this channel. A bird in his garden had first suggested to his mind the unseason-ableness of the month of March, and thence by inexplicable sequence rose the memory of another sort of *march*, that of a long-forgotten composer of the eighteenth century,

I

Charles Avison. The memory thus awakened deepened
and grew, till the echo of the music rang in his ears loud
and clear.   Next came consideration of the question why
the music and musician are alike forgotten.   In his own
day Charles Avison's music supplied all that was needed;
it moved its hearers as forcibly as the music of to-day
moves us.   How then does it come that his name to-day
wakens neither memory nor recognition ?   Browning sets
forth this question very earnestly and clearly, and he
then proceeds to answer it in an equally forcible manner.
In the first place, music appeals to the soul rather than
to the mind, and it evokes feeling rather than thought.
The power and effect of music are therefore as unapproach-
able and as indescribable as the soul itself ; and the re-
production of the workings of the soul is as impossible as
a photograph of the deepest workings of the sea, whose
ebb and flow we note, but know not whence they come
nor whither they tend.   From this relation of music to
the soul, Browning argues that as the soul is imperishable,
so is the effect produced by each successive musician.
Nevertheless the times change, and with each generation
comes the demand for fresh expression of the emotions in
fresh music.   Each century, by the irresistible law of
eternal progress, draws nearer to the aim and end of
music, to

> " . . . . . . have the plain result to show—
> How we feel, hard and fast as what we know."

In this lies the aim and end towards which every Art
aspires and music most nearly touches, but which none
shall altogether reach.   Thus one star wanes and another
rises, but, says Browning—

> " Never dream
> That what once lived shall ever die ! "

They may seem dead, these musicians of the past, they
and their music together ; but a breath from our life will
kindle theirs, and give them power to speak to us to-day
as to those of ages long ago.   The essence of soul and of
music are the same now as then, and Browning's purpose
to-day, as Avison's of old, is man's good simply.   They
will therefore march together, and the music of the past
shall rouse in the poet of the present memories of a yet
more distant past, the connecting link of which shall be
Avison's music with Browning's words to express the
glories of the Commonwealth.   The last stanzas are
accordingly written in metre to an air of Avison's, the
music of which is given at the end of the poem.

The Epilogue, *Fust and his Friends*, opens humorously
with the arrival of the seven friends who have come to
entreat Fust from his evil ways.   They find him in great
dejection, and at once attribute the cause to sin or to remorse.   Accordingly they remonstrate with him, and
even endeavour to exorcise the evil spirit by pious
prayers, in the repetition of which, however, their memories play them sadly false.   Impatient of their chatter,
Fust rushes from the room, promising to return shortly
with a copy of the prayer in which his friends have made
so many blunders, but which he declares he knows by
heart.   He does return after a few moments, throws open
the door of an inner room, and discovers at work the
printing-press, the invention of which he had just completed.   He explains the process, and distributes copies
of the prayer as samples of his work.   After some few
exclamations of incredulity, astonishment, and super-

stitious terror, his friends suddenly realise the perfect simplicity of the machine, and profess to be but little impressed by the invention.

The story is, of course, identical with the legend which attributes the invention of the printing-press to Dr. Faust, and there are several allusions in the poem to the incidents of Goethe's *Faust*. The material difference, however, appears in the fact that, while traditions attribute Faust's invention of the printing-press to his being in league with the evil one, Browning makes it appear as an act of atonement for a hitherto ill-spent life. This idea is presented in a speech, half-prayer, half-thanksgiving, that God has granted him the joy of conferring so great a benefit on mankind. Even as he speaks, however, the thought is borne in upon his mind that, as printing can increase the spread of good and truth throughout the world, so can it diffuse evil and falsehood. The note of sadness which these thoughts arouse is, however, quickly dispelled by the interruption of some of the friends, who again protest that the same thought had struck them at first sight of the apparatus. This barefaced, but withal amusing, announcement is followed by a play upon the word "goose," and the name of Huss, the first reformer, who was supposed at the stake to have foretold the coming of Luther ; and with Fust's confirmation of this prophecy the Epilogue closes.

It may seem strange to many that Browning should have chosen for the recipients of his "parleyings" men so altogether unknown in his own day ; but a moment's reflection shows the wisdom of his choice. Had he chosen more popular celebrities, the interest of his readers might possibly have been increased ; but it would have been interest in the individual, not in the subject on which the poet was speaking.

ASOLANDO ; FANCIES AND FACTS. (*1889. Published Dec. 12th, the day of Browning's death in Venice.*)

It is needless to dwell upon the sad association which must surround this "swan-song" of its great author. *Asolando* is Browning's dying legacy to the public, and is held sacred accordingly. But the poems contained in this latest volume are not all of recent date. Mrs. Orr tells us that in 1887-8 he wrote *Rosny, Beatrici Signorini, Flute-Music, Bad Dreams, Ponte dell' Angelo, White Witchcraft,* and it certainly seems as if the *Prologue, Epilogue, Speculative,* and several others must belong to the latest period. *The Cardinal and the Dog* was written in 1840 for Macready's little son, that he might amuse himself by illustrating the story. Browning explains the title *Asolando* in a dedicatory note to Mrs. Arthur Bronson . . . . "*a title-name popularly ascribed to the inventiveness of the ancient secretary of Queen Cornaro, whose palace tower still overlooks us : Asolare—'to disport in the open air, amuse one-self at random ;' . . . but the word is more likely derived from a Spanish source. I use it for love of the place, and in requital of your pleasant assurance that an early poem of mine first attracted you thither.*"

The *Prologue* dwells upon the disillusionment which comes with age ; but, with characteristic optimism, admits only rejoicing at what thus reveals absolute truth.

Rosny.—A woman laments the death of her lover, who with rash haste "went galloping into the war ;" but her grief seems to be assuaged by the thought that, as he fell dead on the battle-field, her portrait lay on his breast, not that of her rival, Clara, whom she is apostrophising.

Dubiety describes the desire for a state of rest which is not sleep, in which everything is hushed and shaded, yet not obscured. But the repose which the speaker longs for is obviously the calm of old age, beautified by the memory of love.

Now is a lover's rhapsody. In that "moment eternal" when love is first owned mutual, past and future sink into insignificance beside the glory and perfect bliss of the present.

Humility expresses the gratitude of an unsuccessful lover who can rejoice in the smiles which fall on him through the wealth with which love for another has endowed his beloved one.

Poetics. The speaker urges that lovers are in fault to use such terms as "my rose," "my swan," to praise their loved ones. The highest praise there is he can accord his love—

" What is she? Her human self,—no lower word will serve."

Summum Bonum (the highest good). Admirable and wonderful is the vigour of this love-poem, written as it is by a man long past seventy. All the glories of the sea are reflected in the shade and shine of one pearl, in one gem all the wonders of the mine, but greater than both is the truth and trust. . . .

" In the kiss of one girl."

A Pearl, a Girl, is also a love-song. It tells an

Eastern legend that by whispering the right word there is power in a pearl to conjure up a spirit which shall make you lord of heaven and earth. So with the heart of a girl : whisper the right word, and love wakes at the call, and makes you indeed sole "lord of creation."

Speculative is obviously a tribute to Mrs. Browning. It declares that to others heaven may mean some new state, but for the speaker, heaven, could he choose, should be earth with its old joys and sorrows, "so we but meet our part again."

White Witchcraft is a love poem in a more playful strain than usual. The lover suggests that, could he usurp Jupiter's power, and transform his lady love into an animal, and she became a fox, and she changed him into a toad, still she would feel—

" He's loathsome, I allow :

.   .   .   .   .

But see his eyes that follow mine—love lasts there any-how."

Browning's love of animals, etc., has already been mentioned, and it is probable that this reference to the toad is a reminiscence of one of which he made a great pet in youth.

Bad Dreams.—I. describes a man's dream of his love with her "faith gone, love estranged." He woke with two-fold joy : first, that it was only a dream ; and, secondly, because he realised that had it been true, though it had broken his heart, his love would have remained unchanged.

II. is a dream of a strange unseemly revelry in the midst of which the dreamer sees the girl he loves. When he awakes, the dream has so taken hold of him that he muses whether the spirit may not escape at night, and the dream be the reality after all. The girl answers his fear with a laughing retort and description of her dream, which she declares was the fellow of his.

III. is a dream of art and nature, each good in its way, but which result in confusion and chaos when one springs up in the place which should belong solely to the other.

IV. is a dream of a woman evidently treated with neglect and contempt by her lover. She dreams that she is dead, and that then, too late, he visits her grave, heart-broken and remorseful that he had so little appreciated her while she was still with him.

Inapprehensiveness protests against those who allow the head to take precedence over the heart. The protest is illustrated by the story of a woman, who is so occupied in trying to remember the name of a certain author that, standing side by side with the man who loves her, she is quite unaware of his love. The result is that he accepts her on her own ground, and instead of telling her of his love, helps to find the forgotten author.

Which ?—Three ladies are discussing the qualities each thinks noblest in a lover, while " an Abbé crossed legs to decide on the wager." The first requires high thoughts, the second high deeds, while the third will accept the vilest wretch—

" So he stretch
Arms to me his sole saviour, love's ultimate goal."

The Abbé gives unqualified preference to this last as being most pleasing before God.

The Cardinal and the Dog has its origin in the

"Grand Dictionnaire Historique," where the story is told in a slightly different form of a certain Cardinal Marcel Crescentio. On March 25th, 1522, the Cardinal was writing letters to the Pope till late into the night. His work completed, as he rose from his chair, he saw an immense black dog which sprang towards him. Terrified, he called for his servants to drive it away, but they could find no sign of it. The Cardinal, however, was so shaken by the shock that he fell ill and died, the nightmare and terror of the dog haunting him to the end.

The Pope and the Net relates the story of a fisherman's son who was raised to the position first of Deacon, then Priest, Bishop, Cardinal, and lastly Pope. Whilst he remained Cardinal, he had his fisherman's net hung on the palace wall in place of a coat-of-arms. When he became Pope, however, and the people flocked to do him homage, the net was gone. One bolder than the rest ventured to ask the reason—

" ' Why, Father, is the net removed?' 'Son, it hath caught the fish.' "

The Bean Feast.—Pope Sixtus V., wandering disguised among the poor, entered a tumble-down house and found the inmates happily at supper. The people were very poor, and seemed awed at the priest's condescension in searching out their wants. With reassuring words Sixtus threw back his hood and showed he was the Pope. Their consternation increased, and all were at a loss how to repay such goodness.

" ' Thus amply,' laughed Pope Sixtus, 'I early rise, sleep late :

> Who works may eat : they tempt me, your beans there:
>   spare a plate. ' "

The Pope shared the poor folks' meal, then rose and went his way, thanking God that, despite his high place, appetite and digestion of humble fare were nowise destroyed.

Muckle-mouth Meg tells how a young lord makes a raid across the Border and is caught red-handed. His life is offered him on condition of his marrying a girl who is described to him as "Muckle-mouth Meg." He, without seeing her, declines to marry a monster, and is given seven days in a dungeon to think it over. During this time he is waited on by a pretty girl, and falling in love with her, is the more confirmed to prefer death to the marriage offered him. At the week's end he persists in his refusal, and she then tells him that she herself is " Muckle-mouth Meg."

Arcades Ambo [1] is directed against vivisection, to which Browning was strongly opposed.

The Lady and the Painter.—The lady reproaches the painter with inducing a modest girl to stand naked as his model. He defends the practice on the ground that both painter and model are joined in a reverent praise to God for his good gift of beautiful womanhood. On his part he reproaches the lady with the murder of God's innocent birds for the savage decoration of her hat. But they both keep their own opinion.

Ponte dell'Angelo, Venice, relates an amusing legend of how a lawyer got the better of Satan. The lawyer was a grasping, avaricious man, whose extortions were notorious. On one occasion when he could not forget the wails of a

---

[1] Cf. Tray, *Dramatic Idylls*. First Series.

certain widow whom he had robbed, he invited the chief
of the Capucins to dinner, hoping that the presence of
such a holy man might disinfect his house. When his
guest arrives, the lawyer excuses himself for a moment to
see that his servant has everything prepared. This servant, he explains, is an ape; whereupon the priest at once
jumps to the conclusion that the ape must be a fiend in
disguise. He therefore adjures the ape to show himself
in his true form, and forthwith Satan appears. He explains that he has been sent to fetch the lawyer to hell,
but that the man as yet eludes his clutches by never
failing to say a prayer to the virgin before he goes to bed.
The priest then bids Satan vanish, but the fiend says he
dare not leave the house without doing some mischief to
prove that he has accomplished his errand. The priest
therefore suggests that Satan shall depart through the
wall, leaving a gap for all to see. He does so, and the
priest goes down to dinner. The lawyer calls to the ape,
but of course receives no answer. He then sees, to his
horror, that the priest is wringing blood out of his napkin.
He asks the meaning, and the priest explains that it is a
symbol of his wringing gold from his clients; then takes
him upstairs, and shows the gap in the wall. The terrified
lawyer promises to mend his ways, and the priest absolves
him. But the gap in the wall remains, and he fears Satan
might return through it, so the priest suggests that in the
breach through which the devil went out the lawyer should
place the figure of an angel, past which Satan dare not
venture.

"So said and so done. See the angel has place
 Where the devil had passage!"

Hence the name of the bridge.

Beatrice Signorini was the wife of Francesco Romanelli, a painter of Viterbo,[1] in the seventeenth century. Soon after their marriage Romanelli went to Rome to paint, and there became enamoured of Artemisia Gentileschi, a painter. When he was leaving Rome, Artemisia gave him a picture which she had painted. Festoons of flowers surrounded an empty space in which he at once painted her face, thus uniting their arts, since no other union was possible. When at home once more, Romanelli, thinking his Beatrice too placid and meek to complain, showed her the picture. His wife praised and admired the flowers, then stabbed the beautiful face in their midst and stood—

> " In quietude
> Awaiting judgment."

The sight of her jealous love and passion delighted her husband, who was cured of his infatuation for Artemisia in redoubled love and admiration for his wife.

Flute Music, with an Accompaniment.—A man and a woman sitting together hear through the trees the sound of a flute. He fancies that he can hear various emotions of joy, love, and grief in the sounds, but the lady un-romantically tells him the player is a neighbour who spends his hour's leisure from office-work in studying—

> " Youth's Complete Instructor
> How to play the Flute."

Distance has lent enchantment to the sound and altered sharp to flat. The disillusioned man wonders whether it

---

Forty miles from Rome.

is distance (*i.e.* her indifference or shyness) which makes
him think the lady all he could wish.   If so, he begs—

"But since I sleep, don't wake me!"

"*Imperante Augusto Natus Est.*"—The scene of this
poem is laid in Rome during the reign of Augustus, great-
nephew of Julius Cæsar.   Two Romans are waiting to
enter the public bath.   One of them relates how, on the
previous day, tiring of the long Panegyric which Lucius
Varius Rufus had read on the Emperor, he had left the
crowd, and as he walked along he reflected on the great-
ness of Augustus.   A beggar, asking alms, disturbed his
reverie.   As he handed a coin he saw the beggar's face—
it was Augustus.   He then remembered the report that
once a year, to remind himself of the changeability of
fortune, Augustus disguised himself as a beggar and
walked the streets asking alms.   The speaker, too, reflected on the swift changes of this world's fortune,
"Crown now, cross when?"   The poem ends with a
reference to a supposed prophecy of the birth of Christ.

Development tells how Browning at five years old learnt
the history of the siege of Troy from his father, who
illustrated the scene with the help of tables and chairs,
the dogs, page-boy, etc.   Thence grew the desire to read
first Pope's translation and then the original.   The poem
also speaks of his regret when first he learnt that Wolf
(1795) discredited Homer's authorship, and it dwells upon
the beauty and use of illusion.

Rephan again teaches the lesson that our "reach must
exceed our grasp."   The idea of the poem was suggested
to Browning "by a very early recollection of a prose
story by the noble woman and imaginative writer, Jane

Taylor of Norwich." This story tells how an inhabitant of the star Rephan grew discontented with the perfect happiness in the star, and came to earth. When the knowledge of death there came to him, he spent all his life preparing for it.

In the poem the speaker is the inhabitant of Rephan, and he describes life in the star—the peace, plenty, and content. He cannot explain why this perfection did not suffice him; but by some unseen power he felt the need of strife, not rest, and he found only discontent in a " wealth that's dearth."

Reverie asserts the firm belief that Love and Power are one and the same, but they cannot be entirely reconciled on earth because of the incessant necessary conflict between good and evil. *Reverie* contains the last lesson of Browning's religion of love. The two last verses sufficiently express the spirit of the poem :

> " I have faith such end shall be :
>   From the first, Power was—I knew.
> Life has made clear to me
>   That, strive but for closer view,
> Love were as plain to see.

> " When see ?   When there dawns a day,
>   If not on the homely earth,
> Then yonder, worlds away,
>   Where the strange and new have birth,
> And Power comes full in play."

Epilogue is a fitting close to the work and life of Browning. The courage which never failed him is here nobly and beautifully expressed. Added interest may perhaps be lent to the poem by the characteristic remark which Browning himself made upon it. One evening, just before his death-illness, the poet was reading its third verse[1] from a proof to his daughter-in-law and sister. He said: "It almost looks like bragging to say this, and as if I ought to cancel it; but it's the simple truth; and as it's true it shall stand."

[1] Quoted on p. 7.

THE END.

CHRONOLOGICAL TABLE.

The Dates are those of Publication.

1833. PAULINE. A Fragment of a Confession.

1835. PARACELSUS.

1837. STRAFFORD.

1840. SORDELLO.

1841. BELLS AND POMEGRANATES.

No. I.—*Pippa Passes.*[1]

BELLS AND POMEGRANATES.

No. II.—*King Victor and King Charles.*

BELLS AND POMEGRANATES.

No. III.—*Dramatic Lyrics.*

CONTENTS.—Cavalier Tunes: I. Marching Along;[2] II. Give a Rouse; III. My Wife Gertrude. Italy and France.[3] Camp and Cloister.[4] In a Gondola. Artemis Prologizes. Waring. Queen-Worship: I. Rudel to

---

[1] *Pippa's Song*, Part. III., was originally published in the *Monthly Repository*, 1885, as *The King*.

[2] 1863. Re-named *Boot and Saddle.*

[3] 1863. Re-named *Italy—My Last Duchess; France—Count Gismond.*

[4] 1863. Re-named *Camp—Incident of the French Camp; Cloister—Soliloquy of the Spanish Cloister.*

K

the Lady of Tripoli ; II. Cristina. Madhouse Cells, I. and II.[1] Through the Metidja
to Abd-el-Kadr. The Pied Piper of Hamelin.

1843. BELLS AND POMEGRANATES.

IV.—*The Return of the Druses.*

BELLS AND POMEGRANATES.

V.—*A Blot on the 'Scutcheon.*

1844. BELLS AND POMEGRANATES.

VI.—*Colombe's Birthday.*

1845. BELLS AND POMEGRANATES.

VII.—*Dramatic Romances and Lyrics.*

CONTENTS.—How they brought the Good
News from Ghent to Aix. Pictor Ignotus.
Italy in England.[2] England in Italy.[3] The
Lost Leader. The Lost Mistress. Home
Thoughts from Abroad. The Tomb at St.
Praxed's.[4] Garden Fancies : I. The Flower's
Name ; II. Sibrandus Schafnaburgensis. France
and Spain : I. The Laboratory ; II. The Con-
fessional. The Flight of the Duchess. Earth's
Immortalities. Song. The Boy and the An-
gel. Night and Morning, I. and II.[5] Claret

---

[1] 1863. Named—I. *Johannes Agricola* ; II. *Porphyria's Lover.*
[2] 1849. Re-named *The Italian in England.*
[3] 1849. Re-named *The Englishman in Italy.*
[4] 1863. Re-named *The British Bishop Orders his Tomb at St. Praxed's.*
[5] 1863. Re-named — I. *Meeting at Night* ; II. *Parting at Morning.*

and Tokay.[1] Saul. Time's Revenges. The Glove (Peter Ronsard, *loquitur*).

1846. BELLS AND POMEGRANATES.

VIII.—*Luria: A Soul's Tragedy.*

1850. CHRISTMAS-EVE AND EASTER-DAY.

1855. MEN AND WOMEN. In two volumes.

VOL. I. CONTENTS.—Love Among the Ruins. A Lover's Quarrel. Evelyn Hope. Up at a Villa—Down in the City. A Woman's Last Word. Fra Lippo Lippi. A Toccata of Galuppi's. By the Fireside. Any Wife to Any Husband. An Epistle containing the Strange Medical Experience of Karshish, the Arab Physician. Mesmerism. A Serenade at the Villa. My Star. Instans Tyrannus. A Pretty Woman. Childe Rolande to the Dark Tower Came. Respectability. A Light Woman. The Statue and the Bust. Love in a Life. Life in a Love. How it Strikes a Contemporary. The Last Ride Together. The Patriot : an Old Story. Master Hugues of Saxe-Gotha. Bishop Blougram's Apology. Memorabilia.

VOL. II. CONTENTS.—Andrea del Sarto. Before. After. In Three Days. In a Year. Old Pictures in Florence. In a Balcony.

---

[1] 1863. Re-named *Nationality in Drinks.*

Saul. De Gustibus. Women and Roses.
Protus. Holy Cross Day. The Guardian
Angel—A Picture at Fano. Cleon. The
Twins.[1] Popularity. The Heretic's Tragedy:
A Middle-Age Interlude. Two in the Cam-
pagna. A Grammarian's Funeral. One
Way of Love. Another Way of Love.
"Transcendentalism:" A Poem in Twelve
Books. Misconceptions. One Word More:
To E. B. B.

1856. BEN KARSHOOK'S WISDOM.[2]

1864. DRAMATIS PERSONÆ.

CONTENTS.—James Lee.[3] Gold Hair: A
Legend of Pornic. The Worst of it. Dîs
Aliter Visum; or, Le Byron de nos Jours.
Too Late. Abt Vogler. Rabbi Ben Ezra.
A Death in the Desert. Caliban upon
Setebos, or, Natural Theology in the Island.
Confessions. May and Death. Prospice.
Youth and Art. A Face. A Likeness.
Mr. Sludge, the Medium. Apparent
Failure. Epilogue.

---

[1] Written and published in a Pamphlet for a Bazaar in 1854, together with "A Plea for the Ragged Schools of London," by
E. B. B.

[2] Written, 1854, at Rome. Published 1856 in "The Keepsake.'
Never reprinted. To be found in Dr. Furnivall's Browning Bibliography.

[3] Reprinted in Edition of 1868 as *James Lee's Wife.*

1868-69. THE RING AND THE BOOK.   In four volumes.

1871. BALAUSTION'S ADVENTURE : Including a *Transcript from Euripides.*

1871. PRINCE HOHENSTIEL-SCHWANGAU : SAVIOUR OF SOCIETY.

1872. FIFINE AT THE FAIR.

1873. RED COTTON NIGHT-CAP COUNTRY ; OR, TURF AND TOWERS.

1875. ARISTOPHANES' APOLOGY, including a *Transcript from Euripides,* being the *Last Adventure of Balaustion.*

1875. THE INN ALBUM.

1876. PACCHIAROTTO, AND HOW HE WORKED IN DISTEMPER : WITH OTHER POEMS.

CONTENTS.—Prologue.   Of Pacchiarotto and how he worked in Distemper.   At the Mermaid.   House.   Shop.   Pisgah-Sights, I. and II.   Fears and Scruples.   Natural Magic.   Magical Nature.   Bifurcation.   Numpholeptos.   Appearances.   St. Martin's Summer.   Hervé Riel.   A Forgiveness. Cenciaja.   Filippo Baldinucci on the Privilege of Burial.   Epilogue.

1877. THE AGAMEMNON OF ÆSCHYLUS.

1878. LA SAISIAZ.   THE TWO POETS OF CROISIC.

1879. DRAMATIC IDYLLS.   First Series.

CONTENTS.—Martin Relph. Pheidippides. Halbert and Hob. Ivàn Ivànovitch. Tray. Ned Bratts.

1880. DRAMATIC IDYLLS. Second Series.

CONTENTS.—Prologue. Echetlos. Clive. Muléykeh. Pietro of Albano. Doctor. Pan and Luna. Epilogue.

1883. JOCOSERIA.

CONTENTS.—Wanting is—What? Donald. Solomon and Balkis. Cristina and Monaldeschi. Mary Wollstonecraft and Fuseli. Adam, Lilith, and Eve. Ixion. Jochanan Hakkadosh. Never the Time and the Place. Pambo.

1884. FERISHTAH'S FANCIES.

CONTENTS.—Prologue. I. The Eagle; II. The Melon-Seller; III. Shah Abbas; IV. The Family; V. The Sun; VI. Mihrab Shah; VII. A Camel Driver; VIII. Two Camels; IX. Cherries; X. Plot Culture; XI. A Pillar at Sebzevah; XII. A Bean-Stripe; also, Apple Eating. Epilogue.

1887. PARLEYINGS WITH CERTAIN PEOPLE OF IMPORTANCE IN THEIR DAY.

CONTENTS.—Apollo and the Fates. — A Prologue. I. With Bernard de Mandeville; II. With Daniel Bartoli; III. With Christo-

pher Smart ; IV. With George Bubb Doding-
ton ; V. With Francis Furini ; VI. With
Gerard de Lairesse ; VII. With Charles
Avison. Fust and his Friends.—An Epilogue.

1889. ASOLANDO.

CONTENTS.—Prologue. Rosny. Dubiety.
Now. Humility. Poetics. Summum
Bonum. A Pearl, a Girl. Speculative.
White Witchcraft. Bad Dreams: I., II.,
III., IV. Inapprehensiveness. Which ?
The Cardinal and the Dog. The Pope and
the Net. The Bean Feast. Muckle-Mouth
Meg. Arcades Ambo. The Lady and the
Painter. Ponte dell' Angelo, Venice.
Beatrice Signorini. Flute Music, with an
Accompaniment. "Imperante Augusto Natus
Est—" Development. Rephan. Reveri .
Epilogue.

INDEX.

---◇---

152